The New Power of Children and Young People

David Cohen

LONDON AND NEW YORK

Cover image: Getty Images

First published 2023
by Routledge
4 Park Square, Milton Park, Abingdon, Oxon OX14 4RN

and by Routledge
605 Third Avenue, New York, NY 10158

Routledge is an imprint of the Taylor & Francis Group, an informa business

British Library Cataloguing-in-Publication Data
A catalogue record for this book is available from the British Library

Library of Congress Cataloguing-in-Publication Data
A catalog record has been requested for this book

ISBN: 978-0-367-76096-0 (hbk)
ISBN: 978-0-367-76097-7 (pbk)
ISBN: 978-1-003-16548-4 (ebk)

DOI: 10.4324/9781003165484

Typeset in Sabon
by MPS Limited, Dehradun

Contents

The New Power of Children and Young People

In a rapidly changing world, children have more of a voice than ever before. In *The New Power of Children and Young People*, David Cohen explores how this has happened, what the consequences might be and how we can best engage with our young people.

David Cohen considers the social, political and psychological issues involved in children and young people's influence, and how it impacts the balance of power between children and parents and other adults in their lives. It examines crucial topics including the role of high-profile young people such as Malala Yousafzai and Greta Thunberg; their knowledge of and anxieties around global issues such as climate change; children's relationships with technology and social media; their changing relationships with parents and guardians; how children develop a sense of justice; sex and relationships; how children are depicted in TV and film; young people's experience of education; and shines a light on their growing political confidence and engagement.

Young people should be interested as well as parents, teachers, social workers, politicians and other key professionals involved in children and young people's lives. This thought-provoking book offers insight to help us understand young people's lives.

David Cohen is a prolific writer, filmmaker and psychologist.

Introduction

In November 2021 at COP26, Prince William introduced a 15-year-old Indian girl. Vinisha Umashankar invented a solar-powered ironing device after she learned how burning charcoal hurt the health of the "ironing wallahs" and polluted the air. Umashankar called on the greybeards who control the world to give up "old ways and habits." She added that "many of my generation are angry and frustrated at leaders who've made empty promises and failed to deliver." The ironing inventor did not just have science smarts; she was verbal too. "I'm not just a girl from India, I'm a girl from earth. Today I ask with all due respect that we stop talking and start doing," she said at COP26.

Twenty-three-year-old Amanda Gorman had already been young poet laureate of California when she was chosen to recite at President Biden's inauguration. She told *The Wall St Journal* that the role of the poet is "to question and investigate." A romantic view would be that is also the role of the young. Gorman added "If the poet can help us ask the right questions then that points us to the right destinations." For her the most important issue is understanding climate change, working out how to rectify it and, then, taking the necessary actions. Don't "blah blah blah," as that other earth girl Greta Thunberg put it crisply.

Mary Robinson, who had been President of the Irish Republic from 1990 to 1997, insisted at COP26 that she understood the frustration of young people. Barack Obama arrived to say he got why young people were angry and urged them to continue pressing world leaders to act seriously. He sniped at the Presidents of China and Russia who had not bothered to turn up. In China, there are no demonstrations by students and President

DOI: 10.4324/9781003165484-1

Qi has the status of a demigod, and so is never criticised. The Queen is a lesser being by comparison as she is just Supreme Head of the Church of England. Unusually she was caught complaining that politicians tended to talk rather than act. She refrained from saying blah blah blah, perhaps because she only utters well-constructed sentences.

David McClelland, one of the most influential psychologists of the 1960s, developed a theory of achievement. He suggested there were periods when parents read their children books that celebrated achievement and that motivated them to achieve. So were there children's books in the early 2000s that did that? There does not seem to be "Mr Ambitious" in the Mr Men series, let alone "Peppa Pig wins the High Jump." This does not invalidate McClelland's ideas but we perhaps need to study why there are so many high-achieving young today.

The great novelist E.M Forster said, "how do I know what I think till I see what I say." That is very true of this book as the subject of young people and politics is the subject of constant debate, divisions, revisions, demonstrations and confrontations.

The footballer Marcus Rashford never imagined he would change government policy on providing free meals to poor children, but he did just that. Gavin Williamson, the Education Secretary in September 2021, was sacked not just for the failure of his policies, but because he muddled up Rashford with Mar Itoje, a rugby player who has been campaigning for children to get laptops. Rashford and his campaign have now become part of the GCSE syllabus. When accepting an honorary PhD at the University of Manchester, he said it felt "bittersweet" to receive a degree for fighting child poverty the day after the £20 a week Universal Credit uplift was taken away. He added that the government's cuts meant "millions of families across the UK lost a lifeline." He called for politicians to get "out into communities" including Wythenshawe in South Manchester where he grew up. He knew how poverty made people suffer. Prince William in November 2021 pinned an MBE on him.

Malala Yousafzai survived an assassination attempt and won a Nobel Prize for her work on the education of girls. All before she was 18.

In some ways the story would make a good Hollywood epic – Young Heroes. By the end they would solve –

Climate change.

Racism – after the killing of George Floyd, young people co-ordinated action to support filing charges against police in brutality cases and disseminating information about racism in institutions.

Inequality in Latin America and the Caribbean has seen protests for social justice. The social tsunami was accompanied by the thunderous banging of pots and pans used in protests across the continent.

Literacy–in December 2020 three youth organisations demanded more work on literacy.

The Afghan refugee crisis – and every other refugee and migrant crisis too.

The COVID crisis at the time of writing.

It is a pity Bruce Willis is too old to now star as the hero.

Powerful movements usually provoke powerful reactions. At present, perhaps because politicians are ashamed of denying climate change, the reaction comes mainly from two sources – a few countries who do well out of oil and gas and companies who have every interest in arguing that climate change is, well if not a hoax, at least not so dangerous.

Some of the questions this book deals with are factual. How much do young people know about politics? What are they taught in schools? How much do they care? How does this caring translate into action? We have become used to laments about the politics of hatred which prompts the question: how does the expression of hatred affect the young?

Psychology aspires to be a science, but one problem that muddies much research on attitudes is how accurate such measures are. A global industry deals with measuring and understanding attitudes, some political, some commercially vital like which Cola tastes better and which aftershave will make men more desirable. Interpreting the results is beset with methodological problems. The most obvious are do subjects report their own attitudes truthfully and are their attitudes consistent over time and do attitudes change behaviour?

The power between generations is also an important issue. There is an old Yiddish saying, "when a father gives to his son, both laugh; when a son gives to his father, both cry." The saying should include daughters and mothers too. There is startingly little published research on the subject of intergenerational jealousy and the effect of social media – perhaps because techno giants do not really want to probe it too deeply. So it has been left to *Elle* magazine to offer a long piece on the subject in February 2021, which is discussed in Chapter 10.

In this absence of much academic research on intergeneration jealousy, the book offers a speculation. Alfred Adler's theory of the inferiority complex, which described how children felt inferior and some never got over it, has been outlined in Chapter 10. In Adler's day young people did not outdo their parents. Today is different, so chutzpah to the fore, I sketch out a possibly useful new test; the Parental Inferiority Test, also known as the PITs? to stimulate research. Earlier grownups wanted to smack their little ones because the tykes misbehaved; now grownups want to smack them because they can play fantastic algorithms. Discuss, as they say in exam papers.

Serious as the topic is, the book tries to entertain as well as explore the latest relevant research in politics, history and psychology. Young people protesting is hardly new. In 1962 as a teenager, I marched on Aldermaston where the British nuclear programme's research was based. The protesters included the philosopher Bertrand Russell and a young Alan Smithers, whose work on education is reported in Chapter 9. We marched because we feared that some crisis would spiral out of control, as the Cuban missile crisis of 1962 threatened to do. Stanley Kubrick's sharp comedy *Dr Strangelove* satirised this.

Both the bomb and HIV were specific dangers with specific answers. There is no retroviral cure or international treaty that can stop climate change, however. No one has created a Dr Strangelove for our times yet; because, one could argue, the threat to the planet is too frightening, even though there have always been deniers.

Apart from marching to Aldermaston, I cannot claim to have been a campaigner, except in the field of mental health where I have written and made films. Chapter 14 deals with one consequence of the social media multiverse – high levels of stress and suicide in the young. This rise contradicts Stephen Pinker's *The Better Angels of Our Nature* (2011) where he argues that violence in human societies has steadily declined over time. His *Enlightenment Now* (2018) uses social science data to show a general improvement of the human condition over recent history. Pinker bats for rationality, but many do not accept his almost Panglossian view that the world is getting better. Many old crises seem almost intractable, like old sores. When will they ever learn? as Marlene Dietrich sang in 1962.

In 2021, teenagers in Belfast are yet again hurling petrol bombs and setting fire to buses as their fathers and grandfathers did in the 1960s and 1970s.

One cannot write of 1960s Belfast without mentioning Bernadette Devlin. She was born Catholic in County Tyrone. Her father raised her to hold *Irish Republican* ideals; he died when Bernadette was nine years old. The family had to depend on welfare to survive, which affected Bernadette deeply. She was 19 when her mother died, leaving her to help raise her siblings while also studying *psychology* at *Queen's University Belfast.* In 1968 she took a prominent role in a student-led *civil rights* organisation, *People's Democracy.*

Devlin then was elected to the *Westminster Parliament.* Irish Republicans always refused to swear the Oath of Allegiance to the Queen new MPs have to take, but she insisted, "I will take my seat and fight for your rights." Aged 21, she was the *youngest MP at the time.*

The day before her 22nd birthday, she made her *maiden speech.* She remained the youngest woman ever elected to Westminster Parliament until the *May 2015 general election* when 20-year-old *Mhairi Black* became a Scottish Nationalist MP.

The troubles in Ulster led to some interesting research and the paradoxical finding that levels of psychiatric disturbance decreased during the violence. It has been argued that people resort to violence as a result of feeling powerless. The teenagers in Northern Ireland felt their rioting gave them some power and so they were less likely to show mental health problems.

Many societies revere the old because they are assumed to have experience and wisdom. There is a French proverb "*si jeunesse savait, si viellesse pouvait.*" If youth knew, if old age could.

Today it would be harder to argue children and young people do little and do not have much influence. Malala Yousafzai, Greta Thurnberg and Marcus Rashford almost lecture their often tone-deaf elders, who dare not dream of giving them a clout round the earhole as they would once have done. Social media can turn a child or young person into a celebrity, and celebrities get a hearing. No one knows how many "influencers" there are but it is likely that many of them are young. Technology has given the young more of a voice. Half of seven-year-olds in the developed world own a mobile phone. How many have a smartphone?

Give children a voice

In the past, writers like Charles Dickens described how children were exploited, so the idea that children should have a voice is relatively new. Historically, children were meant to be seen but not heard. Rachel de Zousa, the new Commissioner for Children in England, is utterly opposed to such silence. In her first annual report in 2021, she wrote:

> And at the heart of this we must listen to children. 'The Big Ask' will be the largest ever consultation with children in this country. We want to hear from children from every background about how the pandemic has affected them, their hopes and ambitions for the future, and to hear what is holding them back. We will put children's voices at the centre of the Commission. Their views and experiences and ideas will help shape the way we deliver better outcomes not just for them, but for all our children in the decade ahead.

De Zousa will have to be deft and determined to make that happen though, as we shall see TV gives far more space to children and young people's views.

Millionaire kids

Society measures success in terms of money today even more than it did in the past. Forget the scribblers. We are now seeing the rise of young entrepreneurs, some of whom have become millionaires, not through inheriting wealth but making it themselves. The five who follow exclude Prince George who will inherit the throne after Prince Charles and Prince William. The young prince is apparently worth £3 billion without having lifted a regal finger.

The traditional rags-to-riches story used to start with an energetic youth running a stall in some street market as Alan, now Lord, Sugar did. Today Sugar is also an online phenomenon. When she was just 14 Aline Morse set up the cutely named Zollipops which provides sugar-free lollipops to health-conscious Americans in over 7,000 stores. Zollipops is making Zollibucks as the company is on the fast track to making over $6 million in sales in 2022.

When Syed Sumail Hassan was seven years old, he began playing Dota 2. Now he is one of the leading gamers in the world, having won Dota 2 championships with his team "Evil Geniuses," and prize money of more than $6.5 million. In 2016, he was named one of *TIME magazine's* "30 Most Influential Teens" and is currently estimated to be worth at least $3 million.

The Australian Ben Pasternak created several successful social networking mobile apps, including Monkey, Flogg and Impossible Rush. Impossible Rush proved so successful that it even managed to outperform Twitter and Tinder on App Store's top charts. His status as top young dog was cemented in 2016 when he was named one of *TIME Magazine's* most influential teens.

We do not usually think of teenage estate agents. In 2016, Akshay Ruperlia, however, launched an online agency that let new homeowners pay the lowest amount of commission possible. He was still studying for his A levels at the time, but the twin pressures of studying and turning his idea into a profitable operation did not stop him. Today, Ruperlia is worth a massive $12 million.

Visa has just launched a credit card for children and trumpet that it shows children need financial education, but it also targets the very young as a new market. If they had historical sense, they would call it the Napoleon since the Emperor became a general very young and many gold coins are called Napoleons.

To start at the very beginning

I started to write this book in the midst of the COVID-19 pandemic and as concerns about social media heightened. It became clear that Facebook – or should we call it Facemask given critiques of how frank it is? – and other techno giants were unwilling to do enough about sexual and hate messages, and the cloak of anonymity which protects those who post them. The period also saw the tragedy of the deaths of George Floyd and Sir David Amess. The death of the latter prompted many MPs to disclose how much hate mail and death threats they get, which makes it important to address the way the vituperative political debate has affected young people.

The debate is also confusing because there are knowns, known unknowns and unknown unknowns. This adds to the intensity of position taking because admitting you do not know or cannot pin down facts you should know, can make people aggressive, defensive and even abusive. After that platitude consider these two questions;

How many COVID cases are there?

This appears easy to answer, but there are issues.

What is the rate of global warming?

This appears easy too as we are told we need to keep under 1.5% but there is no agreement about the extent of global warming. Is it 1.1% or 1.28%?

Uncertainty causes anxiety and makes people take up fixed positions.

Leon Festinger's theory of cognitive dissonance suggests people will seek evidence that confirms their beliefs in an attempt to ward off anxiety (Festinger, 1957). As early as 1987, Heissen et al. warned that some individuals may avoid and resist learning about computers due to their anxiety. These authors developed the Computer Anxiety Rating Scale (CARS) by examining the behavioural, cognitive and affective components of computer anxiety. Higher levels of computer anxiety were related to greater math and test anxiety, and to less computer experience and mechanical interest.

More savvy less deference

We are in a brave digital new world where children and young people are often better able to cope with the technology and social media that shapes much of our lives. This makes some parents feel inadequate. Even in the simpler past, parents were sometimes jealous of their children. That is more likely now, when a ten-year-old may well be more familiar with all the apps, Snapps and Wapps and know how to play complicated computer and video games. Dad and mum are all too often dummies. As a result, children and young people have more of a voice than ever before.

We are also seeing the decline of deference. We no longer live in a world where the workers doff their hats to the ruling class or where the young do not question the old and do as they say. I return to the subject later.

This book argues that the balance of power between children and parents is changing and explores the consequences. A century ago in *The Wasteland* T.S. Eliot wrote that "A crowd flowed over London Bridge." Commuters are still flowing over the bridge when they go to work and then go home at night. In 1922, however the commuters were pretty much all white. Today they are diverse in every way. Few sport the bowler and brolly. The world pulses with diversity. And if we do not mind the way we discuss that we may be cancelled.

The New York Times noted that over the last 19 months, "a large number of Americans have left cities, their marriages and organized religion. Some have recently tried dumping social media. It seems that many see 2021 as a year to finally leave prepandemic lives behind and embrace the idea of a fresh start."

Perhaps the most pronounced example is what economists are calling "The Great Resignation."

People gave up jobs in health care, education, retail, food services and child care, sometimes even walking out in the middle of a shift.

There was a mix of reasons. People fretted about getting COVID at work, and had "better unemployment benefits, and savings built up during the pandemic that make it easier for them to turn down jobs they don't want, or which don't pay a living wage. For the first time in decades, many workers across the income spectrum have some leverage, and they are using it to demand better pay and superior working conditions."

The psychology of the pandemic may be playing a role. Surveys suggest that the crisis led many people to rethink their priorities. Behavioural scientists say times of disruption and transition create new opportunities for growth and change.

Staying the course, whether in an unfulfilling job or an unhappy relationship, can also cost you, as Lindsay Crouse and Kirby Ferguson in Opinion wrote:

> "Despite what many of us were taught in childhood – that quitters are losers – there can be significant penalties to passively remaining in place, particularly in the form of missed opportunities. For example, research has shown that one of the best ways for women to increase their salaries is to quit their job and find a new one."

Thoughtful quitting, Lindsay and Kirby argue, may actually increase the power of individuals.

"I'm not saying quit everything. Lots of great things require perseverance – our relationships, our health, our careers," Lindsay said. "But think about it: perseverance shouldn't be a default, it should be a choice."

Express your fears, repress your fears is a sentence Freud would have understood. In the wake of the 1914–1919 war, he argued that humankind had a death wish. If we do not deal with the climate crisis properly, it would confirm that theory. In 2015, the Mommyish website declared it was amazed toddlers survived because they indulged in so many dangerous behaviours such as jumping off chairs and touching knives. Far more seriously, children and young people do not seem immune, as suicide and attempted suicide statistics suggest.

As this book explores a number of subjects it may be useful to offer an outline of chapters.

The structure

Chapter 1 – A Brief History of Significant Children deals with young people through history who have made an impact. A stellar cast whose impressive women includes Mary Queen of Scots and Greta Thurnberg.

Chapter 2 – Research on Political Participation looks at work which explores the contradictions on the subject of the political involvement of young people. Much of this is based on surveys. The main trends have not changed much over years. Young people today care perhaps even more than earlier generations but vote less often

Chapter 3 – Personality Research and the Big Five Model looks at personality research and how that impacts these issues. There is some interesting work on the personality of young people who become activists.

Chapter 4 – COP OUT - The Illusion of a Future, Young People's Anxieties analyses what makes children and young people anxious and too often suicidal. The chapter looks at fears about COVID-19 and climate change as well many cases where students kill themselves. One puzzle is that protests about suicide tend to be local.

Chapter 5 – "And That's Not Right!" Children's Sense of Justice returns to psychology from reportage. It looks at the work of Jean Piaget, which is still key though many psychologists have criticised it. His views on the moral development of children remain a good basis from which to study young people's ideas about justice.

Chapter 6 – Children, Family and Politics looks at the family and the areas where young people today have more expertise than parents and the consequences of that. If a ten-year-old is more tech-savvy than Mum and Dad, how does it affect their relationship?

Chapter 7 – Technoference: Or How Technology Warps the Bonds between Parents and Children covers the so-called technoference. The more you spend time on screen, the less time for human relationships – what is the impact of that on relationships between parents and children?

Chapter 8 – The Paradox of Tech-savvy and IQ examines the paradox of techno-savvy and IQ. The level of IQ has been falling in recent decades, which seems peculiar given young people are more skilled technologically. I offer a possible explanation.

Chapter 9 – Children as Victims Too examines the dark side as it were. Children and young people may have more power now but there are many instances where they are victims. Since the 1960s, many organisations including the Taliban have recruited children as soldiers. Some of these fighters are just ten years old. The experience scars them. The chapter also looks at the sexual exploitation of children and how they are often used as slave labour.

Chapter 10 – Fairy Tales and Children's TV: Weak Children Who Become Strong considers a paradox. Fairy tales often tell the story of powerless children who triumph over obstacles and so discover who they are and what they can achieve. At their most positive, social media give young people a way of communicating their ideas and feelings, but as we shall see– hence the paradox – using social media carries risks.

Chapter 11 – The Challenge to Education looks at education. It highlights two questions. How have social media and the use of computers changed the classroom? And then how much politics are young people taught? In the United Kingdom surprisingly little, in the U.S.A there is a programme to teach civics but only a quarter of states seem to do so.

Chapter 12 – Sex - Children Are More Knowing, but More Exploited, Than Ever covers sex, especially the question of how the political power of young people affects their sexual behaviour.

Chapter 13 – The Parental Inferiority Complex offers a new complex, the Parental Inferiority Complex. If your children are smarter than you are, how does it change your relationship with them?

Chapter 14 – Emotional Intelligence and Politics looks at emotional intelligence, how children develop it and its effect on political attitudes.

Chapter 15 – Mental Health and Technology looks at how social media use affects mental health and the response of techno giants to the issue.

Chapter 16 – The Typical Child 2046 tries the risky but enjoyable (for the author at least) way of predicting the future and asks where research should probe.

I set out to write a mix of research and reportage not any kind of polemic. The book should interest not just academics, but teachers and all who work with children.

I also hope it will interest parents – and here again the developed world at least is changing. In 2018, the U.K. Office of National Statistics showed that the average age of mothers having their first child was 30.6 years, while the average age of new fathers was 33.6 years. This is the tenth consecutive year that this number has increased. A generation ago mothers on average had their first child when they were 24 years old.

The shift has been reflected among some of the world's most high-profile women. The Duchess of Sussex was 37 when she gave birth to baby Archie, while Amal Clooney was 39 when she had her twins. Recently a number of celebrities have become fathers in their 60s and even older. John Humphrys, who presented the today's programme on the BBC's Radio Four, became a father again in his 70s. So we have older parents and more savvy children. Summon the therapists.

This book tries to explore this changing landscape so it covers psychological research as well as politics. It reports on a number of surveys carried out between 2018 and 2021. Events do change attitudes but there is a general drift. Many young people are anxious; they feel let down by political leaders who prate about improving the state of the world but do as little as they can. But the right place to start is with the history of children who made, and are making, a difference.

Chapter 1

A Brief History of Significant Children

Rao was first influenced by a science kit her uncle gave to her when she was four years old. When she was ten, Rao heard about the Flint water crisis and became interested in ways to measure the lead content in water. She developed a device called *Tethys* which could send water quality information via Bluetooth. She won the Discovery Education 3M Young Scientist Challenge and was awarded $25,000 for her invention. *Tethys* contains a 9-volt battery, a lead sensing unit, a bluetooth extension and a processor. It uses carbon nanotubes, whose resistance changes in the presence of lead. She presented her idea at the 2018 MAKERS conference and raised a further $25,000.

Rao was awarded the United States Environmental Protection Agency President's Environmental Youth Award. She also got the Top "Health" Pillar Prize for the TCS Ignite Innovation Student Challenge in May 2019 for developing a diagnostic tool called Epione based on advances in genetic engineering for early diagnosis of prescription opioid addiction. As if that is not enough, she is working on getting her pilot's license.

In 2020, Rao became the first person to receive *TIME magazine*'s Kid of the Year designation.

If there were magazines in ancient Egypt, Tutankhamen who became Pharaoh when he was nine would surely have been on the cover of Nile News.

Then in 85 BC, after his father died suddenly, Caesar became the head of the family at 16. His coming of age coincided with a vicious civil war between his uncle Gaius Marius and Sulla. Marius was in control of Rome when Caesar was named as the new *Flamen Dialis* (high priest of Jupiter). It was his first important post.

DOI: 10.4324/9781003165484-2

He went on to conquer most of Europe till he was murdered. As this book marries the serious and fun, it should be noted that his murder inspired one of the immortal comic lines in a Carry On film.

As he dies Caesar, he says "infamy, infamy, they've got in for me."

Over a thousand years later in 1212, The Children's Crusade began in spring. Thirteenth-century chroniclers called them "pueri," Latin for children. In 1977, the Dutch historian Peter Raedts argued that the Latin word referred not only to those who were children, but also to those who were socially "small." In other words, pueri could be peasants. The word infants, however, also appears in the sources describing participants in the crusade: this term refers unequivocally to children.

Henry III was three when he became king in 1216 and, though he was not a "great" king, he did manage to get the support of Pope Honorius who ruled that the Papal legate should protect Henry and his kingdom – mainly from the French. Wisely, Henry took the cross, declared himself a *crusader* and so entitled to special protection from Rome. Then Henry gave Louis of France the vast sum of £6,666 to speed his departure from England and promise to try to persuade King Philip to return Henry's lands in France. Not bad for a young King.

Henry believed that kings should rule England in a dignified manner, surrounded by ceremony and ecclesiastical ritual. His predecessors had allowed the status of the Crown to decline. He adopted King *Edward the Confessor* as his *patron saint*, hoping to emulate the way in which Edward had brought peace to England and reunited his people in harmony.

Henry also allowed a great innovation. He let Parliament agree upon the raising of taxes. During his reign, the counties began to send regular delegations to these parliaments and came to represent a broader cross-section of the community than simply the major barons.

Mary Queen of Scots was just a year old when she became the Queen of Scotland. An English diplomat, *Ralph Sadler*, saw the infant at Linlithgow Palace in March 1543 and wrote, "it is as goodly a child as I have seen of her age, and as like to live."

As Mary was an infant she had to have regents rule in her name. From the outset, there were two claims to the regency: one from the *Catholic Cardinal Beaton*, and the other from the *Protestant Earl of Arran*, who was next in line to the throne.

King Henry VIII of England grabbed the opportunity of the regency to propose a marriage between Mary and his own son and heir, *Edward*, hoping for a union of Scotland and England. The *Treaty of Greenwich* was signed, which promised when she was ten, Mary would marry Edward and move to England, so Henry could oversee her upbringing.

The death of Henry VIII in 1547 caused turmoil. Mary's guardians, fearful for her safety, sent her to *Inchmahome Priory* and turned to the French for help. King *Henry II of France* proposed to unite France and Scotland by marrying the young queen to his three-year-old son, the *Dauphin Francis*. Arran also winkled a French dukedom for himself and agreed to the marriage.

When she was five Mary was sent to France. She was especially tall by 16th-century standards (she reached the height of 5 feet 11 inches or 1.80 m), while Henry II's son and heir, Francis, stuttered and was unusually short. It did not matter. Henry commented, "From the very first day they met, my son and she got on as well together as if they had known each other for a long time." On 4 April 1558, Mary signed a secret agreement bequeathing Scotland and her claim to England to the French crown if she died childless. Twenty days later, she married the Dauphin at *Notre Dame de Paris*, and he became king consort of Scotland.

After the Dauphin died, Mary made the mistake of fleeing to England after she had been implicated in a number of murders. She expected her cousin Elisabeth I to protect her. The story of how Good Queen Bess had her executed instead has been the subject of plays, films and books including one which pitted Glenda Jackson as Elisabeth against Vanessa Redgrave as Mary. It featured scenes where the two women met, when in fact Elisabeth always refused to see Mary.

Mary's son James inherited the Scottish throne and, when Elisabeth died in 1603, the English throne in 1603. He made an interesting contribution to the literature. He wrote a book for his son giving him advice on how to be king. Among much else, it warned a king always had to be on his guard against flattery, eat daintily and pray constantly to keep his soul pure.

As the absolute power of the monarchy declined after the fall of the Stuarts, the office of Prime Minister became vital. One of its early holders was young indeed. In 1783, William Pitt became Great Britain's youngest Prime Minister ever. He was only

24 years old. The contemporary satire, *The Rolliad*, ridiculed him for his youth:

> Above the rest, majestically great,
> Behold the infant Atlas of the state,
> The matchless miracle of modern days,
> In whom Britannia to the world displays
> A sight to make surrounding nations stare;
> A kingdom trusted to a school-boy's care.

Many saw Pitt as a stopgap but his government lasted 17 years.

The student revolt of 1968

The most memorable example of young people demanding more political power was in 1968, the year of the student revolts in Europe. A leading figure Daniel Cohn-Bendit was born in 1945 in *Montauban*, France, to *German Jewish* parents who had fled *Nazism* in 1933. In 1966, he went to study sociology at the *University of Paris' Faculty in Nanterre* and soon joined the nationwide *anarchist* federation, *Fédération anarchiste*. He left in 1967 in favour of the smaller and local *Groupe anarchiste de Nanterre* and the *Noir et rouge* magazine.

When in May 1968, student and workers riots erupted in Paris against *Charles de Gaulle*'s government, Cohn-Bendit quickly emerged as a public face of the student protests. Not all leftists applauded. The French Communist Party leader *Georges Marchais* described Cohn-Bendit as the "German anarchist Cohn-Bendit" and denounced some student protesters as "sons of the upper bourgeoisie ... who will quickly forget their revolutionary flame in order to manage daddy's firm and exploit workers there." Continued police violence, however, prompted trade unions (and eventually the Communist Party) to support the students, and from 13 May onwards, France suffered a general strike.

However, Cohn-Bendit had already retreated on 10 May with a few friends to *Saint-Nazaire*, seeing that his Nanterre group had become a minority without political influence in the larger Paris students' movement. His political opponents took advantage of his German passport and had him expelled from Saint-Nazaire to Germany on 22 May as a "seditious alien."

Though Cohn-Bendit had participated little in the May 1968 Paris events, he had become a legend. He returned to *Frankfurt* in the family house and became one of the co-founders of the *Revolutionary Struggle* (*Revolutionärer Kampf*) in *Rüsselsheim*. He worked in the *Karl-Marx-Buchhandlung* bookshop in Frankfurt and ran an anti-authoritarian *kindergarten*. In his 1975 book *Le Grand Bazar*, he described himself as engaging in sexual activities with very young children at the kindergarten. In 1978, an edition of *Pflasterstrand,* an alternative magazine Cohn-Bendit edited, described being seduced by a six-year-old girl as one of the most beautiful experiences the author had ever had. In 2001, Cohn-Bendit said that the accounts were invented for purposes of "verbal provocation," and that "I admit that what I wrote is unacceptable nowadays."

In 1984 he joined the *German Green Party*. Four years later he published, in French, *Nous l'avons tant aimée, la révolution* (in English: *We Loved It So Much, the Revolution*), a book full of nostalgia for the 1968 counter-culture and announced his shift towards more centrist policies. In 1989, he became deputy mayor of *Frankfurt*, in charge of multicultural affairs. Immigrants made up some 30% of the city's population at that time. He also developed a more tolerant policy towards drug addicts.

Today Cohn-Bendit describes himself as retired though, he is involved in making television programmes including one on Brazil and football and one on Israel.

When I spoke to him, he was very measured in assessing the impact of 1968. He stressed it was unwise to speak of the young as any kind of a unified block. He pointed out first of all that historically the young had not always been on the side of progress. During the Nazi regime, the majority of students had supported Hitler. Today the intervention of young people in politics is mixed. In Germany, many of them supported the far right. Yet 1968 had changed the social and cultural climate. "It's complicated," he said. Chou En Lai, Mao tse Tung's second in command was asked what the consequences of the 1789 French Revolution were, he replied with splendid inscrutability that it was too early to tell. I suspect Cohn-Bendit might agree in terms of the consequences of 1968. I also asked him what his relationship was with that other key figure of 1968 – Tariq Ali. He said that politically they had never been close because Tariq was a Trotskyite.

Tariq Ali

Tariq Ali was born and raised in *Lahore*, Punjab in *British India*. He first became politically active in his teens, taking part in opposition to his country's rulers. An uncle who worked in Pakistani military intelligence warned his parents that Ali could not be protected. They decided to send him to Oxford where he studied *Philosophy, Politics and Economics*. He was elected President of the *Oxford Union* in 1965 where he met *Malcolm X* in December 1964 who told him he was afraid of being assassinated.

As time passed, Ali became increasingly critical of *American* and *Israeli foreign policies*. He marched on the *American embassy in London* in 1968 in a demonstration against the *Vietnam war*.

In 1967, Ali was in *Camiri, Bolivia*, not far from where *Che Guevara* was captured, to observe the trial of *Régis Debray*. He was accused of being a *Cuban revolutionary* by authorities. Ali then said, "If you torture me the whole night and I can speak Spanish in the morning I'll be grateful to you for the rest of my life."

Ali has been described as "the alleged inspiration" for the *Rolling Stones*' song "*Street Fighting Man,*" recorded in 1968. *John Lennon*'s "*Power to the People*" was inspired by an interview Lennon gave to Ali.

Neither Cohn-Bendit nor Tariq Ali achieved serious office or became billionaires. One can hardly discuss influential young people without discussing Mark Zuckerberg and Bill Gates who were technology pioneers and prodigies before they were 20.

Two teenage titans

Mark Zuckerberg was born in White Plains, New York, on 14 May 1984, the son of psychiatrist Karen (née Kempner) and dentist Edward Zuckerberg. He and his three sisters were raised in a Reform Jewish household. His great-grandparents were Jewish emigrants from Austria, Germany and Poland.

He had a *Star Wars*-themed bar mitzvah. It would be wonderful to have a video of that ceremony. He was also academically excellent. On his college application, he stated that he could read and write Ancient Greek, French, Hebrew and Latin. He was captain of the fencing team too. Did that make him combative?

Zuckerberg's father taught him Atari BASIC Programming in the 1990s. His father's dental practice was operated from their home, he built a software program he called "ZuckNet" that allowed all the computers between the house and dental office to communicate with each other. It is considered a "primitive" version of AOL's Instant Messenger, which came out the following year.

Zuckerberg has said, "I had a bunch of friends who were artists. They'd come over, draw stuff, and I'd build a game out of it." The *New Yorker* piece noted that Zuckerberg was not, however, a typical "geek-klutz."

The Napster co-founder Sean Parker, a close friend, notes that Zuckerberg was "really into Greek odysseys and all that stuff," recalling how he once quoted lines from the Roman epic poem *Aeneid*, by Virgil, during a Facebook product conference.

The *New Yorker* noted that by the time Zuckerberg began classes at Harvard in 2002, he had already achieved a "reputation as a programming prodigy." He studied psychology and computer science. In his sophomore year, he wrote a program that he called "CourseMatch," which allowed users to make class selection decisions based on the choices of other students and also to help them form study groups. A short time later, he created a different program he initially called "Facemash" that let students select the best-looking person from a choice of photos. According to Arie Hasit, Zuckerberg's roommate at the time, "he built the site for fun." Hasit explains:

> "We had books called Face Books, which included the names and pictures of everyone who lived in the student dorms. At first, he built a site and placed two pictures or pictures of two males and two females. Visitors to the site had to choose who was "hotter" and according to the votes there would be a ranking."

The site went up over a weekend, but by Monday morning, the college shut it down, because its popularity had overwhelmed one of Harvard's networks and prevented students from accessing the Internet. Many students complained that their photos were being used without permission. Zuckerberg apologized publicly.

In January 2004, Zuckerberg began writing code for a new website. On 4 February 2004, Zuckerberg launched "Facebook."

Zuckerberg dropped out of Harvard in his sophomore year to complete his project. In January 2014, he recalled:

I remember really vividly, you know, having pizza with my friends a day or two after – I opened up the first version of Facebook at the time I thought, "You know, someone needs to build a service like this for the world." But I just never thought that we'd be the ones to help do it. And I think a lot of what it comes down to is we just cared more.

Bill Gates was already a mogul by the time Facebook was born. He had discovered computers at the highly selective Lakeside School in Seattle, which then had a rented PDP-10. He and his childhood friend Paul Allen made his first computer program there: a game of tic-tac-toe (tic-tac-toe).

In 1968, aged 13, Gates founded the Lakeside Programmers Group with Allen and a few other friends. In 1973, he entered Harvard University at the age of 18. There he met Steve Ballmer, future CEO of Microsoft. He quickly abandoned his studies.

Bill Gates' first success was to co-produce a BASIC interpreter for the Altair 8800. This achievement is both a tour de force and a stroke of luck: the development is done entirely on PDP-10 and the Altair BASIC is only tested on a real Altair 8800 on the day of the demonstration, which succeeds perfectly. The Altair BASIC marks a milestone in the history of microcomputing: it will be the first programming language to run on a commercial microcomputer. It will also be the first software published by the company Microcomputer Software, founded for the occasion. Microsoft became the world leader as Windows became the main programme personal computers use.

None of today's young stars have become as powerful as Gates and Zuckerberg – yet.

In power now

One king who is still reigning is Oyo in Uganda. He came to the throne aged three, after his father died in 1995. For his coronation, he sat on a miniature throne and played with toys after a mock battle with a grownup "rebel" prince. At one point, His Majesty dashed from the throne to climb onto his mother's lap. He also yanked off a lion-skin crown that was too heavy for his little head.

The next day, King Oyo attended a meeting with Cabinet members who were old enough to be his grandparents.

"The first few years, I did not know what was going on," he says. "I think I realized when I was about 6 that I really was king, and my life was going to be different. I was going to have responsibilities toward a lot of people."

King Oyo now oversees a Cabinet that includes a prime minister, board of regents and councilmen.

Some young people achieve power in zones of conflict.

Vsoje Osmani was born in 1982 in Mitrovica. Her political career began in her teens. On 27 August 2009, she was elected Chief of Staff of the then President of the Republic of Kosovo, *Fatmir Sejdiu*. Osmani was a member of the Kosovo Assembly for three terms. As well as *Albanian*, she also speaks *English*, *Turkish*, *Spanish* and *Serbian*.

I am grateful to her for giving me time to interview her.

The writer Lawrence Durrell worked as a diplomat in the Balkans and his book *Esprit de Corps* gave a hilarious account of his adventures in the Balkans around 1950. Yugoslavia was the dominant country and it was ruled by Marshal Tito who had led the resistance against the Nazis during the Second World War. Tito was a Communist but not the kind of lackey Stalin liked. After Tito died, Yugoslavia split into a number of countries. Some were mainly Christian, some Muslim. The Balkan war of 1995 saw a number of atrocities, the most infamous being the massacre at Srebenitsa.

Osmani grew up in very troubled times. "No one chooses to be a refugee." Her experience of being a refugee herself marked her. "Being a refugee makes you see the value of life and the value of compassion," she told me.

"I followed politics it was impossible not to do so. Listening to the news all the time." She was obviously very intelligent – not a characteristic shared by all Presidents – and "I had always had the ambition to study in the States or Britain."

I asked her if she was political as she grew up.

"In a formal way no but in a non formal way every family was political. After Milosevic in 1989 invaded Kosovo CHECJ, there was a movement which included all the Albanian families." Her family was Albanian and the movement aim to help Kosovo achieve freedom and independence.

"I won a scholarship. It was always a dream to finish my studies in the States." She managed to do that and lived for a while in Pittsburgh. She taught there for some years and got her doctorate there. "It was an excellent experience."

Kosovo declared its independence in?

I asked her if being a woman had been a disadvantage. She countered "it makes me better, Politics is not an easy activity for women anywhere. It takes working more hard men to get recognition. It's a hard and bumpy road."

Kosovo was profoundly a patriarchal society when she began. "Kosovo has really emancipated and women can do the job really better. We are more compassionate and principled. Statistics show that women in politics are not involved in corruption."

She sees the future as dealing with domestic challenges. Kosovo has a high level of unemployment. She also sees dealing with the consequences of the pandemic which has led to unemployment. She also wants to see her country developed in music, sports and cultural activities.

Internationally, she added, "We face many challenges. Russia has in Serbia a client state and there have been tensions on the border." So far these have not led to actual fighting.

So 23 years after independence she opened the borders of her small country to allow Afghan refugees to pass through on their way to the West. "No matter how small we are we can help out."

Hope is a word she likes.

As a university professor, she taught International Law in Kosovo, while in America "State Building and Law: The Kosovo Experience." She served as the representative of Kosovo at a case in the *International Court of Justice*, where she defended the legality of the *independence of Kosovo*.

She was seen as a possible *Prime Minister of Kosovo* in the 2019 election. While campaigning she said that she believed that the Kosovan people were ready for a female Prime Minister, and that she could fight corruption, as well as promising free-market reforms for Kosovo.

Osmani has published books, articles, monographs and papers in the field of International and Commercial Law, in both Albanian and English. She discussed The Role of Parliamentary Diplomacy in Shaping the Foreign Policy of the Republic of Kosovo; University of Pittsburgh, Law Review, except publication: FALL, 2014, Kosovo's foreign policy: Five Years On (in "Political Thought: Foreign Policy and Aspects of International Diplomacy," co-author; 2011, No 43, September 2013; Konrad Adenauer Stiftung) and representing Kosovo before the International Court of Justice; Centre for International Legal Education (CILE Notes), September 2010, University of Pittsburgh School of Law.

Osmani is being proactive in the Afghan crisis. She has negotiated a deal with the United States. Refugees will be allowed into

Kosovo either to stay or to be processed by American immigration officials. On Newsnight of 18 August 2021, she appeared as a figure of true authority using her experience of being a refugee.

In December 2021, **Gabriel Boric won Chile's presidential election to become the country's youngest ever leader.** The 35-year-old former student protest leader defeated his far-right rival José Antonio Kast by 10 points.

Mr Boric told supporters he would look after democracy, promising curbs on Chile's neoliberal free-market economy.

He will lead a country that has seen mass protests against inequality and corruption recently.

Mr Boric's victory prompted celebrations on the streets of the capital Santiago, with his supporters waving flags and honking car horns.

In his speech, Mr Boric said he was taking on the job with humility and a "tremendous sense of responsibility," vowing to "firmly fight against the privileges of a few."

Greta Thunberg

The career of Greta Thunberg highlights the new power of children. In 2018, she was one of the winners of the competition organized by the newspaper, *Svenska Dagbladet,* offering young Swedes to write an article on the climate for young people. She described her fear of global warming there.

In a letter later, she explained that this competition allowed her to be contacted by "a group of people, especially young people, who wanted to do something about the climate crisis."

On August 20, 2018, the day she returned to the *ninth year* in a school in *Stockholm*, Thunberg started a strike in front of the *Riksdag*, the Swedish Parliament, and told journalists that she would not go at school until *the general elections* of September 9, 2018. Sweden had just experienced a *heat wave* that caused unprecedented *forest fires*. She demanded that the Swedish *government* reduce *carbon dioxide emissions*. She sat in front of the Swedish Parliament every day during school hours. She called for a "school strike for the climate."

After the election, she continued to demonstrate every Friday. The strike attracted the attention of the media of the planet. Children in other countries followed suit including *the Netherlands*, *Germany*, *Finland*, *Denmark*, *Luxembourg*, *France*, *Spain* and *Australia*.

On 15 March 2019, she said on Facebook:

> "We need a new way of thinking. The political system that you adults have created is only competition. You cheat as soon as you can because all that matters is winning. We must cooperate and share what remains of the planet's resources in a fair manner." She has become a role model for her age group and irked President Trump, who liked to call climate change "a very expensive hoax." Although President Biden has reversed many of his policies, Thunberg knows she will be disappointed. "The things that they are going to present will not be nearly enough for what science is saying will be in line with the Paris Agreement," she said. "So, I'll just be calling that out, I guess."

In 2021 a three-part BBC documentary followed her as she took a year off from school to visit sites that show the climate crisis in all its complexity – melting glaciers in the Canadian Rockies, a California town torched by wildfires, a Polish coal mine. The film provides a gentle portrait of Thunberg growing up and growing into her power. She attends the World Economic Forum, in Davos, and confronts the not so good and not so great. She meets with Angela Merkel, the German Chancellor, to discuss the country's Paris Agreement progress, and emerges unimpressed. "Is this in line with what you have promised?" Thunberg asks in the film. "The fact is no."

Thunberg is on the autism spectrum, and argues the condition actually helps her. "I don't follow social codes," she said. "Everyone else seems to be playing a role, just going on like before. And I, who am autistic, I don't play this social game." She eschews empty optimism. "If we humans would actually start treating the climate crisis like a crisis, we could really change things," she said.

Her uncompromising words can give the wrong impression. "People seem to think that I am depressed, or angry, or worried, but that's not true," she said. Having a cause makes her happy. "It was like I got meaning in my life."

"People say autistic people can't understand irony," she went on. She disputes this energetically. "I am irony, almost," she said. "I think the world, as it is, is quite funny." She finds the climate crisis darkly comic, especially the response in rich countries – the posturing, the self-justification, the bargaining, the denial. "If you are doing everything you possibly can, and you can't do anything more, then you might as well just sit back and laugh at it," Thunberg said. "Because otherwise you will get depressed." At COP26 she refused to address the great and the good and stood outside with protesters who cheered her like the star she has become.

Child prodigies

Thunberg could be called a child prodigy, not always a happy label. John Stuart Mill's breakdown was a 19th-century warning about being stuffed with too much knowledge. William James Sidis was a mathematical prodigy. He had a bleak life after Harvard: he self-published speculative manuscripts on the second law of thermodynamics and obsessively collected streetcar transfers.

Today's political child prodigies are not lone voices as they usually have advisers of all kinds. Thunberg does not work alone but is backed by a team. This may seem a little cynical, but such support is necessary as the work of the psychologist Julian Stanley shows. On 1 September 1971, he started the Study of Mathematically Precocious Youth (SMPY) at Johns Hopkins University.

In an interview for the New Scientist, Stanley explained to me that the very first talent search was held in March 1972; 450 Baltimore grade 7 and 8 students took the SAT-M (School Aptitude Test-Math), which had previously only been taken by students in grades 11 and 12. This testing method proved to be very successful in identifying intellectual talent and offering support for social and emotional development too. Zuckerberg attended a number of sessions.

In 1975, a symposium at Johns Hopkins gathered 31 distinguished delegates who were optimistic about teaching children mathematics but warned more than a few were a bit lazy taking their talent for granted. Stanley has been followed by others.

Stanley's work has its followers. Rusczyk founded Art of Problem Solving – or AoPS – in 2002. He offers online instruction in mathematics that's more complex than that in standard gifted-and-talented programs. Some of his videos have garnered hundreds of thousands of views; occasionally, they feature his alter ego, a gravelly voiced character in dark shades and a black hoodie. He is playful.

In 2012, he began rolling out Beast Academy, an elementary-school curriculum in which advanced mathematical concepts are communicated to young math geeks by wisecracking comic-book monsters. By 2019, about 36,000 math students from around the world were using its paid online curriculum or in-person courses, and tens of thousands more were consulting its textbooks for independent study.

Will today's young leaders manage well?

It will be interesting to follow the careers of the following. I rang William Hill to find out the odds they offer on –

Marcus Rashford to become an MP.
Greta to become prime minister of Sweden.
Malala to become Secretary General of the United Nations.
Readers take a punt. I am going to place £5 on each of these.

Chapter 2

Research on Political Concerns and Political Participation

Why do teenagers become more politically engaged?

Neurophysiology may help explain why some of the young become so passionate about politics. By the time children are six, brains are already about 90–95% of adult size. The missing 10% is crucial and stops the teenage brain from being able to function as an adult brain. Jean Piaget (1932) argued that the last stage of cognitive development is that of formal operations where young people can master the intricacies of logic. Bradmertz and others (1999) found Piaget was over optimistic, however. Less than a fifth of us get to that stage.

The underlying physiology has provoked some controversy. Till recently it was believed that during adolescence the brain grew and, when unused, connections between brain cells were "pruned away." Yes, the brain is a rose bush. This pruning begins in the back of the brain. The front part of the brain, the prefrontal cortex, lags behind. This part of the cortex is responsible for our ability to plan and think about the consequences of actions, solve problems and control impulses.

With the frontal cortex not quite operating at full speed, teenagers rely more on the amygdala and the limbic system to make decisions. These are ancient structures that owe much to the reptilian brain. Someone opposed to teenage activism could snipe, "Why you're behaving like a crocodile or dinosaur" though that might be unwise and get themselves cancelled. The amygdala is associated with emotions, impulses, aggression and instinctive behaviour.

One eminent psychiatrist, Daniel Siegel, clinical professor of psychiatry at UCLA School of Medicine, has studied the teenage

DOI: 10.4324/9781003165484-3

brain in detail. As a father of two children who are now in their 20s, "I wanted to understand what happened to them in adolescence. As a clinician, an educator, and a scientist, I was intrigued by new discoveries in the science of brain development that have been made in the past five to ten years. These discoveries directly contradicted some of the popular beliefs, myths, and false statements about adolescence, like teens have 'raging hormones' or are 'lazy' or 'out of control' – negative stereotypes which are really destructive not only to adolescents themselves, but to parents and teachers as well."

Old theories of the brain viewed the prefrontal cortex, at the forward part of the frontal lobe, as simply not mature until the end of adolescence, and that the "immaturity" of the brain explained "immature" teenage behaviour.

Siegel argues this is not consistent with what research is showing us, which is that adolescence is an important, necessary phase and that the restructuring changes that occur then enable new abilities to emerge. Perhaps most important is that many of the brain's changes during adolescence involve increasing the levels of integration between the different parts and functions of the brain, letting neuron speak unto neuron better than before.

Those unpruned parts of the brain become quicker, more coordinated and more effective. Siegel waxes lyrical as he says this architectural restructuring allows the adolescent mind, "which is wonderfully creative, adaptive, and vibrant," to emerge. But research on the neurological underpinnings of post-traumatic stress order identifies the amygdala and hippocampus as key brain areas involved in the registration of potentially dangerous situations and in the later formation of memories.

Neurophysiology helps understand the attitudes of young people, I suggest.

What do we know about young people and politics?

Disraeli, who was Prime Minister twice, knew more than a thing or two about attracting and bamboozling voters, would urge critical caution as one tries to understand the research on young people and politics.

Every political party in Britain and Europe uses social media to reach voters – and especially young voters.

The most thorough research on social media in the United Kingdom comes from Ofcom, the body that regulates the communication industry. Its 2020/21 report found that a third of boys aged 8–15 who admitted they have been bullied said it was via online gaming, compared to one in ten for girls. Parental concerns about in-game spending and gaming-related bullying increase every year. Parents emphasise two particular issues: the pressure on their children to buy things and services, and the possibility of them being bullied through online games.

The last four years have seen an increase in the number of children claiming to have seen hateful material online about particular groups of individuals based on their gender, religion, disability, sexuality or gender identity. We shall see, however, that children can also be bullies.

In 2018, more than half of parents of children who went online believed that the benefits of the internet outweighed the risks for their child. However, the proportion of parents who feel this way has declined from 65% in 2015 to 55% in 2019. Belief that online benefits outweigh online risks increases with the age of the child; 43% of parents of 3- to 4-years old think this is the case, compared to 63% of 12- to 15-years old.

Facts are hard to find

In Britain, we are used to a daily score of COVID cases and COVID- related deaths. There is an astonishing difference between sources of data between the government's figures and others, however. Kings College London conduct a study, led by Tim Spector OBE, Professor of Genetic Epidemiology, which consistently differs from the so-called official figures.

The ZOE COVID figures of new symptomatic cases are based on reports from around 750,000 weekly contributors. One of those 750,000 explained to me that every morning he receives a reminder to report how he feels, whether he has had any symptoms and often, even if he has reported, a further reminder.

At the time of writing, the latest survey figures were based on data from 42,795 recent swab tests conducted between 9 October and 23 October 2021. There were 92,953 new daily cases of COVID in the United Kingdom on average, an increase of 14% from 81,823 new daily cases last week.

The ZOE incidence data are always a week ahead of the other surveillance surveys and continue to work as an early warning signal. ZOE's predicted long COVID incidence rate currently estimates 1,490 people a day will go on to experience symptoms for longer than 12 weeks.

"The ZOE figures are consistently higher than the official confirmed daily cases because we get results from various sources, including self-reported lateral flow tests that are under-reported officially. The government raw figures report on PCR testing of the classical symptoms only, which miss around 40 percent of cases. ZOE extrapolates the data from our sample to predict daily infections in the wider population. With the confirmation of our estimates from the ONS' fortnightly survey, it's clear the government figures are a big under-estimate, and with the highest rates in Western Europe, there's no room for complacency," Spector commented.

The discrepancy – for those who know about it – provokes the question. Is the government hiding the true spread of COVID?

The fear that information is being concealed again provokes anxiety.

What do surveys reveal?

Hundreds of companies in London alone offer to design and administer surveys to find out what people think and how they will behave. The first opinion poll is generally considered to have been held in July 1824. *The Harrisburg Pennsylvanian* asked voters (which at the time meant only men, mostly white and mostly property owners) their opinions on the presidential election due that November.

Before long, many newspapers across the United States were running their own polls. Later in the 19th century, some efforts were made to make the polling more representative. The *Columbus Dispatch* seems to have been the first to use trained interviewers to gather information, and sought a balance of age and occupation among those surveyed.

Most modern polls owe much to the American George Gallup. He pioneered sampling a randomly selected, statistically average group of people. His first poll, in 1932, correctly predicted a local election in Iowa. Four years later, he went against a more respected straw poll conducted by *the Literary Digest*, which saw more than two million people return surveys. Gallup predicted Roosevelt's opponent, Alf Landon, would win. In the event Roosevelt won by a landslide.

Opinions and attitudes change but the findings of many surveys on politics and climate change since 2016 are fairly consistent. Anxiety about nuclear holocaust lessened as the Unites States, the Soviet Union and other nuclear nations limited testing through the Salt Treaty. HIV caused anger and anxiety in the 1980s but then doctors found ways of containing it. COVID has also caused anxiety, rather rationally, as it has killed over three million women and men in 18 months. However, it is not a threat to the very existence of our planet. Climate change could destroy the world. In 2021, for example, rivers in Madagascar dried up leaving its people in the south suffering killer droughts. Politicians in Bangladesh worry 40% of the country will be under water. Rising sea levels will drown island states like the Maldives.

With those possibilities it is not strange that many surveys find that young people tend not to trust politicians and feel alienated from political structures. Not trusting does not mean not caring though. Teixeria in *The Disappearing American Voter* (1992) wrote that levels of participation were steadily declining and that young adults were the most apathetic. He suggested two different reasons. First, the costs of voting are "exceptionally high and the benefits exceptionally low" and second, the lack of voting participation in the younger generation creates a cycle of apathy because young adults feel as though they have no say in government. As a result, many of them choose not to participate in elections.

Patterson (2002), pushed this apathy theory further. Older generations, who were raised during wars, were being replaced by younger generations who are "less politically interested and informed than any cohort of young people on record."

Gentry (2010), in *Why Youth Vote: Identity, Inspirational Leaders, and Independence*, sets out the process a young adult likely goes through when deciding to become active in politics. First there is individual questioning, then the young take actions to discover or confirm an identity and then decides the role that politics will take in her or his life. Identity – how you define yourself – has become a central issue and a tricky one. It has become more fluid than ever before. Do you define yourself as male, female, binary, straight, gay, bi? Freud once told a woman that the fact her son was homosexual was not a sign of any disease. As often he was ahead of the times. Once being gay was seen as sick and sinful, but now it is normal, and even chic.

Winchester et al. (2014), in *Young Adults and Politics: Investigating Factors Influencing Voter Decision Making,* compared a voter deciding who to vote for with a consumer deciding what to buy. Face-to-face interviews suggested that most young adults are not that involved in making political decisions, so they relied on passive information seeking. They were more likely to be influenced by political advertising and interpersonal communication, as compared to loyal voters who will always turn out. If a camel stood for the Conservatives in a safe seat like Richmond, in Yorkshire the voters would duly tick his or her box without, sorry, getting the hump.

Kiousis & McDevitt (2008) added that because of young adults' low interest in politics, they are more likely to be influenced by the small amounts of political information they see. An interview in which President Biden seems lost for words loses more votes than any policy papers. They also argue that most young adults are not likely to pay attention to politics without a trigger like an election, national or local. Once they begin focusing, their opinions are crystallized towards more allegiance to a party. They form these opinions based on agenda setting in the media and the salience of ideas in their environment.

House of Commons research

Some of the most thorough research comes from the House of Commons. In a 2021 briefing paper it defined and summarised the results. In the United Kingdom, political disengagement is more prevalent among certain groups than others. Young people are less likely to register to vote, to actually vote, to be elected and to participate in political activities, but older people tend to have more negative attitudes about politics.

Falling levels of voter turnout and trust in governments across Western democracies are worrying. The proportion of people in Britain who trusted the Government to put the needs of the nation first decreased from 38% in 1986 to 17% in 2013. Trust in politicians has been fluctuating around 9%, according to British Social Attitudes data.

While voting and trust have fallen, levels of political engagement in the United Kingdom appear much higher. These include campaigning, demonstrating and petitioning. And often as we shall see some of these actions show some dramatic flair.

The political scientist Paul Webb argues that there are two types of politically disengaged groups in Britain: dissatisfied democrats who are educated, of higher social status, believe in democracy and have high expectations of what can be achieved, but who are dissatisfied with current politics and want more opportunities to participate. He calls the second group stealth democrats because they are far less active.

Jennings, Stoker and Twyman also differentiate between different types of political disengagement, driven by different beliefs, for example that politicians cannot make a difference; do not tell the truth about difficult decisions or serve the interests of the rich and powerful. They conclude that young people often tend to think politicians and their behaviour are the problem, rather than the political system.

Hands in the till, hands up the skirt – scandal galore

It is not surprising young people are disenchanted with politicians. The list that follows is worrying, but also entertaining as it mainly highlights lust, lucre and sometimes ludicrous attempts to cover them up. Many have been turned into films and TV series. A scandal in 1909 involved Alaska and coal. Later ones involved sex. In 1963, Secretary of State for War John Profumo had an affair with Christine Keeler to whom he had been introduced by the pimp and drug-dealer Stephen Ward. She was having an affair with a Soviet spy at the same time. Keeler's life has been made into a film.

In 1976, the Liberal Party leader Jeremy Thorpe was tried for allegedly paying a hitman to murder his lover, the model Norman Scott, while walking his dog on Exmoor; the hitman only shot the dog, Rinka. Thorpe was forced to resign. It is not clear if the public was more upset by his under the duvet gay affairs or the killing of a dog, Hugh Grant starred as Thorpe in a fine TV series.

There are also stars for crassitude, if that is a word. Jo Moore, within an hour of the September 11 attacks on New York, sent an email to the press office of her department suggesting, "It's now a very good day to get out anything we want to bury. Councillors' expenses?" Since the catastrophic collapse of the towers, the phrase "a good day to bury bad news" (not actually used by Moore) has been used to refer to other instances of attempting to hide an item of bad news behind something worse.

In 2009, the mother of Parliaments turned out to conceal the mother of all fiddles. Members of the British Parliament were exploiting allowances, employing wives as secretaries and were up to every dodgy under the sun, including building a moat at the taxpayers' expense. Dishonourable behaviour by the honourable members.

In 2010, the Chief Secretary to the Treasury, David Laws, resigned from the Cabinet after *The Daily Telegraph* newspaper published details of his claiming around £40,000 in expenses on a second home owned by a secret partner between 2004 and 2009. It was quite against the rules. Laws became the shortest-serving minister in modern British political history with less than 18 days at his desk as a Cabinet Minister.

Since then, there have been allegations of bullying against John Bercow, the Speaker of the House of Commons; and other MPs, David Cameron, the Prime Minister, and Nick Clegg, his deputy in the 2010 coalition, have faced criticism. Cameron lobbied for a company he worked for to be given lucrative contracts; Clegg left to become Vice President of Facemask, sorry Facebook, sorry Meta, as it has rebranded itself. The name has caused derision in Israel as the word "meta" means dead.

In 2021, Owen Paterson had to resign after allegations that he was paid to lobby. Then Sir Geoffrey Cox, who had been Attorney General, was criticised for representing the British Virgin Islands. As a result, he had to spend a lot of time in the Caribbean rather than in the Commons.

It may sound bad, but Britain is seen as a less corrupt country than most. Take the incorrigible French. Nicolas Sarkozy, the ex-President, has been sentenced to jail for bribing a judge. Jacques Chirac, a previous President, nearly got banged up too. Ehut Olmert, the Prime Minister of Israel, was jailed for corruption and Benjamin Netanyahu faces trial on similar charges. In South Africa, President Zuma, who seems to have had an obsessive fear of being poisoned, has been jailed too. The Austrian Chancellor Sebastian Kurz has had to resign though he is not yet behind bars. Surely it is time to revive the facilities on the remote Atlantic island St Helena, where Napoleon lived out his days, as a jail for convicted politicians. An optimist could counter these scandals are positive as in "proper" dictatorships the dictator stays free and rampant.

The Britain Thinks survey confirmed the young's distrust of politicians. A total of 1,026, 18- to 24-year-olds, were critical of the state of Britain. They placed identity issues near the top of the issues they cared most about. Twenty-seven per cent prioritized the rights of Black and minority people. Twenty-three per cent highlighted gender issues making them more important than poverty and inequality. Thirty-eight per cent said they personally knew someone who described themselves as transgender or non-binary. Sixty-eight per cent said they would offer support if a member of their family wanted to change gender.

Off the pedestal

In the culture wars, statues even have become contentious. There has been much debate about the statue of Cecil Rhodes at Oriel College Oxford. He endowed the college with profits from African mines whose workers were exploited. In Bristol, the statue of Edward Colston was pulled off its pedestal and sunk in the harbour. He had been a slave trader. Focus groups showed half the under 25s believed it was right for those who had been involved in the slave trade to have their statues removed, but one subject – only identified as Jacob who lives in Bristol – said, "Having the statue there for me made people learn about it. I learnt how the entirety of Bristol was built with slaves. Although the statute may glorify someone who was a racist, I could also say that those statues still serve a purpose."

Some have even recommended pulling down statues of Winston Churchill because while he saved the world from Hitler, he did express what we now call racist attitudes.

Only 31% of the subjects in the Britain Thinks survey were optimistic about Britain's future while 61% were negative. A nice touch was to ask subjects to compare the country to a person. One said Britain was a shambles and so the best person by way of comparison was Boris Johnson. He has failed to recruit a good hairdresser hence the "shambles." More seriously this may explain why mental health is one of the top three issues for the young, Shimshon, the founder of Britain Thinks, found that far more people – 58% – are optimistic about their own futures than about the country. Yet 55% felt they would have fewer opportunities in life as adults than their parents. Confusion is one theme of the times. Shimson added,

> "perhaps the one lesson the under 25s should learn is that their children will one day think they are out of touch."

Another recent survey from the University of Bath found most young people worried and angry about the future. It questioned 10,000 young people, aged 16–25 years, in the United Kingdom, the United States, Australia, Brazil, Finland, France, India, Nigeria, the Philippines and Portugal. Overall, 75% said, "the future is frightening." In some countries, it was even higher. In Portugal, it was 81%, and in the Philippines, 92%.

Mitzi Tan, a 23-year-old Philippina, explained her history, "I grew up being afraid of drowning in my own bedroom. Society tells me that this anxiety is an irrational fear that needs to be overcome – one that meditation and healthy coping mechanisms will 'fix.' At its root, our climate anxiety comes from this deep-set feeling of betrayal because of government inaction. To truly address our growing climate anxiety, we need justice."

More than 50% of respondents said they felt "sad, anxious, angry, powerless, helpless, and guilty" about climate change. Forty-five per cent said that worry about climate change was affecting their daily lives and how they coped. Fifty-nine per cent described themselves as extremely worried, while 84% said they were moderately worried.

The survey was the first to link young people's concerns to governmental inaction – 58% of respondents said governments are "betraying me, future generations, [or both]."

Governments were failing young people, said 65% of the respondents, while 33% said that the government was not "protecting me, the planet, future generations, [or both]."

Dr Matthew Schneider-Mayerson, an associate professor of Social Sciences and Humanities at Yale NUS College in Singapore, pointed out to *Medical News Today* that "most countries are gerontocracies, run by people in their 60s, 70s, and 80s. They tend to be less concerned about climate change." He argued they may not truly understand the full gravity of the climate crisis. "Hopefully, youth climate activism can put pressure on them to take the kind of action that is urgently."

Global Youth – the largest survey

The Global Survey on Youth & COVID-19 interviewed 12,000 young people from 112 countries, aged between 18 and 29.

Conducted during April and May 2020, the findings are the closest we have to a snapshot of how school closures, lockdown restrictions and the economic slowdown affected young people's lives, learning and livelihoods.

One in six young people stopped working since the pandemic, including those who have lost their jobs and those still employed but working zero hours. Almost a quarter of 18- to 24-year-olds who were working before the pandemic has stopped, compared to just 13% of the 25 to 29 age group. Sectors such as clerical support, service industries and sales were hard hit by business closures and job losses.

Two-fifths of those surveyed viewed their future career prospects in an optimistic light, with more men than women reporting being confident. Slightly fewer people looked ahead with uncertainty, while 16% expressed fear for their career prospects. Thirty-five per cent of young people reported feeling optimistic about the future some of the time, and the same percentage expressed these feelings often or all the time. These surveys suggest there is a large pool of young people ready to protest actively though only a minority take part in normal politics. Academic research confirms these trends.

In some countries, there is no longer normal politics and protesting is dangerous.

Hong Kong – dissent means jail

Students and young people in Hong Kong have led much of opposition to China's attempt to enforce its will. It is very striking in a society where elders have been respected.

Hong Kong's Basic Law came into effect with the 1997 transfer of sovereignty from the United Kingdom to China. Now the Chinese have enacted a security law.

"We don't know exactly how the law will be implemented, but just the perception and uncertainty that it creates will be a problem for the universities," said Sun Kwok, a Hong Kong-born astronomer who was dean of science at the University of Hong Kong for ten years.

The law was imposed by the Beijing government after months of demonstrations in Hong Kong. The protests were initially triggered by a proposed extradition bill that could have subjected Hongkongers to the mainland's legal system. As often, one issue led to a spiral. Protesters then worried about the erosion of the city's quasi-independent status. The law gives authorities new powers to punish "*offenses of secession, subversion, organization, and perpetration of terrorist activities, and collusion* with a foreign country or with external elements to endanger national security" in the Hong Kong Special Administrative Region.

Although the law specifically calls for continuing the policy of one country, two systems that grant Hong Kong a high degree of autonomy and individual rights, university officials fear it will make it more difficult to recruit top faculty and students from outside the city. "We will have a hard time convincing future recruits that they will have complete academic freedom to teach and do research," Kwok added. He is now at the University of British Columbia, Vancouver, in Canada. "In the last 15 years, Hong Kong universities have made huge progress and are increasingly recognized as major centres of excellence in Asia. Can we maintain this gain?"

Many are sceptical. The law "is a retrograde step for Hong Kong," according to Matthew Evans, an ecologist and dean of science at Hong Kong University. Although he is "not expecting a huge impact on what we do" in the faculty of science, he predicts that in the social sciences, law and other disciplines, "people whose research or teaching could fall foul of the law will be self-censoring." And there is likely to be an impact on recruiting, even for the sciences.

Others fear the law could have more direct effects on research. Bruce Lui, a lecturer in journalism at Hong Kong Baptist University, noted that China's concept of national security extends to writing about economics. Scholars might have to tread softly if reporting, for example, inflation statistics that might embarrass the government. One of the oddities of the crisis is that the Hong Kong stock market continues to thrive.

Peter Baehr, a professor of social theory at Lingnan University, pointed out that the mainland government pushes to tinker with the dissemination of certain research results. He said this was seen recently in "the draconian actions against labs that, and persons who, published the genome of the [COVID-19] coronavirus on open platforms."

What you can teach under a repressive regime is a real concern. "Will there be a push for a stronger focus on disciplinary teaching, away from liberal education?" Kwok asked. "There have been voices in certain political circles in Hong Kong that liberal education is to blame for the student unrest in 2019." Expressions of support for the law from university administrators are evidence that already "only those people supporting Beijing can be leaders in the university sector."

Many critics would only speak anonymously before pronouncing the one country, two systems principal dead. "I believe we need to wait before coming to that very serious and in my view tragic conclusion," said one foreign scientist who asked not to be identified. He added that the law's lack of detail and questions about the consequences of violating it are leading to rampant speculation that is inflamed by international media coverage. As a result, "Anyone who is able to leave is probably considering it seriously," he says. The United Kingdom says the law has prompted it to ease immigration rules for more than three million Hong Kong residents eligible to gain UK residency.

The unrest in Hong Kong shows young people willing to risk much for their beliefs. George Orwell would recognise the situation there as being a modern version of 1984 as Big Brother quashed all opposition. The leading paper of dissent, *Apple Daily*, stopped publishing. The law has sliced away the city's freedoms and created a human rights emergency, according to Amnesty International's 30 June, briefing, *In the Name of National Security*. It details how the law has given the Hong Kong authorities free rein to criminalise dissent, while stripping away the rights of those it targets.

Yamini Mishra, Amnesty International's Asia-Pacific Regional Director, said:

> "In one year, the National Security Law has put Hong Kong on a rapid path to becoming a police state and created a human rights emergency for the people living there."
> "From politics to culture, education to media, the law has infected every part of Hong Kong society, and fomented a climate of fear that forces residents to think twice about what they say, what they tweet and how they live their lives."
> "Ultimately, this sweeping and repressive legislation threatens to make the city a human rights wasteland increasingly resembling mainland China."

China's government has repeatedly used "national security" as a pretext to justify censorship, harassment, arrests and prosecutions.

The so-called human rights safeguards set out in the NSL are effectively useless.

People charged under the law are presumed guilty rather than innocent which allows the courts to deny them bail unless they can prove they will not "continue to commit acts endangering national security." An estimated 70% of those prosecuted under the law are currently being held in custody after having been denied bail.

Between 1 July 2020 and 23 June 2021, police arrested or ordered the arrest of at least 118 people for breaching the law. As of 23 June 2021, 45 are presently in pretrial detention.

The Amnesty briefing also outlines how the authorities have used the NSL to crack down on international political advocacy, arresting or ordering the arrest of 12 individuals for "colluding" or "conspiracy to collude" with "foreign forces" because they were in contact with foreign diplomats, called for sanctions from other countries or called for other countries to provide asylum for those fleeing from persecution. Others were targeted for their social media posts or for giving interviews to foreign media.

The law targets alleged acts of "secession," "subversion of state power," "terrorist activities" and "collusion with foreign or external forces to endanger national security." This sweeping definition of "national security" has been used arbitrarily as a pretext to restrict the human rights to freedom of expression, peaceful assembly, association and liberty, as well as to repress dissent and political opposition.

The law's arbitrary application and imprecise criminal definitions make it impossible to know how and when the authorities might deem it has been violated.

Hong Kong may now be Chinese but there is still a legacy of British rule. British judges preside over some courts – and have accepted this new law and done little to defend their fellow judges. One Hong Kong judge, Sham Siu-man, acquitted 12 defendants who faced charges relating to the protests. He was vilified by the pro-Beijing media. In *the Times*, Alistair Carmichael, who chairs Parliament's Hong Kong group, wrote the law is being applied retrospectively though Beijing promised not to do that, "with Hong Kong judged fleeing and legislation being used to silence dissent, however, the time has come for British judges to step back from this parody of justice." It has yet to happen.

Amnesty closed its Hong Kong office at the end of October 2021.

Protests and participation

Britain got a 150-year lease on Hong Kong in 1842, when it defeated the Chinese in the opium wars. At the time Britain itself was in some turmoil. The Chartists marched for better working conditions and more democracy in the 1840s. Then the Suffragettes agitated for the right of women to vote. One of their tactics was to chain themselves to railings. The most dramatic incident was when Emily Davison, who had been arrested on nine occasions, had been on hunger strike seven times and was force-fed forty-nine times went to Epsom for the Derby in 1913. Bravely, she walked on to the course as the race was being run. She positioned herself so that she was hit by King George V's horse Anmer. She died of her injuries.

Recent research has highlighted new ways of protest. In 1973, Robert Dahl, in "*Poliarchy: Participation and Opposition,*" declared political participation was an essential part of modern democracies. For him and Verba and Nie (1972) political participation is "*those activities by private citizens that are more or less directly aimed at influencing the selection of governmental personnel and/or the actions they take.*" Participating can consist of voting, campaign activity, marching, contacting public officials and cooperative activities. Any such activity must be voluntary and observable.

In the 1970s, the women's movement took root. Since then new ways of participating have appeared using non-political behaviour to express political opinions. García-Albacete (2014) argues that these changes characterize today's political participation "repertoire." First, "*the agencies or structures through which citizens are mobilized and participate have (…) been transformed, with the spread of new social movements and advocacy.*"

Before the internet there was no online participation obviously. Researchers now debate how and if online participation fits into existing concepts (Kristofferson et al., 2014). Authors, such as Morozov (2009), declare participation is an illusion while Rojas and Puig-i-Abril (2009) see it as "*expressive participation,*" which constitutes a "*subdimension*" (Rojas and Puig-i-Abril, 2009, p. 907) of political participation. Theocharis (2015) warns that the concept of political participation could be stretched too far.

van Deth (2014) has offered a distinct concept, which should enable researchers to "*recognize a mode of participation if [they] see one.*" To "*see one,*" researchers should look for these characteristics: it is an activity; it is voluntary and not ordered by a ruling class or required by law; it involves people as non-professionals or amateurs; and it concerns government, politics or the state.

In the United Kingdom if 10,000 citizens sign a petition it must be debated in Parliament. There have been petitions on all manner of subjects including the treatment of pets!

These developments show political participation cannot be defined in a simple way. Research needs to adapt and to do so nimbly and fast. One can filet out some trends from the last two decades of work.

What we know about protests and participation

Cammaerts et al. (2014) found that poor participation in the United Kingdom, France, Spain, Austria, Finland and Hungary was due to the existing structure of the political systems and the ways issues were debated; adolescents mainly felt excluded from that. In her research on municipalities in the United Kingdom and the Netherlands, Timmerman (2009) found that neither country made it easy for young adults to participate in debates or the democratic process. Hooghe and Stolle (2003) found that adolescents in Germany, France and the United Kingdom were less likely to vote or participate through institutionalized means than adults, though they were often willing to march or participate in informal ways.

Quintelier, (2007) wrote, "*the low political participation rate among youth is a by-product of their narrow conception of politics and their impression that politicians do not truly care about their needs.*" If young people are not that engaged with politics, it does not mean they are not enraged about some issues. But the organization of politics does not cater to them often. Rainsford (2017) concluded that "*it seems as if the problem of youth political participation is less a matter of whether they participate, and more a matter of where they participate.*"

Evidence in the United Kingdom suggests young people do not get that involved with the youth branches of the main political parties. In general, their membership is low. You get more of a crowd even at a second division football match. The Young Conservatives were once an excellent way of young bloods and fillies meeting. I put it that way given the class background of young Tories who often love hunting, riding and shooting. The organisation needed a transfusion after various scandals and in 2018 the party announced at its spring forum it was relaunching a youth branch under the original name "Young Conservatives." Today there is little evidence that many young have joined.

Young Labour has had its share of problems too. Its membership has been reckoned to be 7,000. These are hardly massive figures.

Single-issue politics

Generation generalisations are always risky, so the following summary needs to be judged with care. "It's the economy stupid," was Bill Clinton's snappy slogan which helped him defeat George Bush Snr. Clinton himself was then defeated by George Bush Jnr. The cynical view, that we vote with our wallets, seems less true of the young partly because the young often do not bother to vote.

One exception was the Scottish Independence Referendum in 2014 when 16- and 17-year-olds were given the right to vote and 89% of all citizens of them did so. The Scottish example shows how the young are often more enthused by single-issue politics (Henn and Foard, 2013).

The British Social Attitudes report (Curtice and Ormston, 2015) revealed that in 2013 only 57% of the respondents felt that they have the duty to vote, compared to 76% in 1987.

The predominant view in the literature is that social class and educational history predict political engagement. The length of time a person has been in full-time education has a crucial impact on their political participation.

Most researchers assume that family has some influence, but they still do not know how much of an influence that is. Studies from Finland (Koskimaa and Rapeli, 2015) and Belgium (Quintelier, 2015) show that school has an influence, without being the most central one. Peers also matter as it has even been shown that "*peers, through discussion and diversity, are even more influential and successful in creating greater political participation*" (Quintelier, 2015, p. 65) than the family. The media are also relevant here especially with the influence of social media which are marked by less distinct boundaries between non-political and political activities, thereby lowering the thresholds of political engagement (Ekström and Shehata, 2018).

Psychology has used twin studies for nearly a century to tease out the role of heredity and the environment. Many studies (Bouchard and McGue, 2003; Alford et al., 2005; Hatemi et al., 2011; Kudrnac and Lyons, 2017) have all looked at the development of attitudes and values amongst twins or parents and their offspring either when they stay with their parents or when they are brought up in different households. "*If father and mother both hold a highly intensive just-world belief, the probability that their child will also hold a strong belief in a just world is very high*" (Schönpflug and Bilz, 2009, p. 229).

Despite shared genes, there are differences between parents and children. Young adults are less interested, more negative and that they don't trust political elites as such (Quintelier, 2007). As Rekker et al. (2015) have shown, longitudinal studies reproduce the same result: Younger cohorts are less conservative on cultural issues but not on economic issues. Eckstein et al. (2012) also mention a key issue of the entire field:

> (...) there is still a lack of studies explicitly investigating young people's orientations toward political behaviours over a longer period of time in order to depict development. Furthermore, longitudinal studies that did account for changes revealed no coherent pattern of results. (Eckstein et al., 2012, p. 491)

Eckstein et al. (2012) demanded more longitudinal studies in this field.

Espinar-Ruiz and Gonzalez-Rio (2015) have shown through large surveys that there is a significant relation between forms of political participation and time spent on the internet though this may not be true for Greece of all places. *Theocharis* has argued that "while the online realm is more likely to cultivate a post materialist mindset, it is also the case that this mindset seems to go hand in hand with a genuine disinterest in political participation."

The current literature is inconsistent as few studies cover new modes of participation thoroughly, which is not surprising as new kinds of social media develop fast. There is also the problem of the lack of larger cross-national studies. In Europe, there is an enormous amount of data available but there is no unified theoretical foundation for studying "European" youth political participation.

A snapshot summary. Young people are anxious and yet optimistic. Only some however become politically active.

Chapter 3

Personality Research and the Big Five Model

There has been some useful research on the personality of activists. Fiske (1949) and Tupes and Christal (1961) proposed the five-factor model, which has become an influential framework for organizing and understanding personality traits. We have seen, among much else, the development of personality inventories designed to assess the five factors through self-report (McCrae and Costa, 1987), the discovery of the five factors in omnibus personality measures such as the Personality Research Form and the Adjective Check List and the empirical demonstration of substantial longitudinal consistency in personality traits within the five-factor framework.

The five broad factors of (I) Surgency (Extraversion), (II) Agreeableness (Warmth), (III) Conscientiousness (Will), (IV) Emotional Stability (Neuroticism) and (V) Culture (Intellectance, Openness to Experience) seem general and emerge from self-report and peer report measures. They feature in a wide variety of standard systems for personality description, including Cattell's 16 factors, Eysenck's "big three," Murray's 20 needs, Guilford's temperaments, Jung's types and the psychodynamic descriptors contained in Block's (1961) California Q-Set. The five factors seem to indicate many of the characteristics that need further study.

Goldberg (1990) argued that a good test is to ask at least five types of questions about a stranger; (1) is X active and dominant or passive and submissive (Can I bully X or will X try to bully me)? (2) Is X agreeable (warm and pleasant) or disagreeable (cold and distant)? (3) Can I count on X (Is X responsible and conscientious or undependable and negligent)? (4) Is X crazy (unpredictable) or sane (stable)? (5) Is X smart or dumb (How easy will it be for me to teach X)?

DOI: 10.4324/9781003165484-4

John (1989) stated that the five-factor model represents "the accumulated knowledge about personality as it has been laid down over the ages in natural language" (p. 269). For him, the five-factor taxonomy is to personality what the Linnaean kingdoms of "plant" and "animal" are to biology – the highest-order classification for all relevant phenomena.

In an extensive study, Soutter and colleagues (2020) found that openness was consistently highly correlated with pro-environmental attitudes and behaviours, as were Agreeableness and Conscientiousness. For Extraversion, only the facets of Activity Level and Cheerfulness were significantly associated, however. It seems that a liking for stimulation lubricates pro-environmental behaviours. An encounter with the police in a demonstration may be rough and nasty but it is also stimulating, after all.

One interesting finding is that Artistic Interests was consistently the strongest associate of pro-environmental attitudes and behaviours. The artist is an outsider, to use a cliché, and outsiders relish taking on authority.

Intelligence also had a comparatively strong association. It makes sense; the more intelligent one is the more one will understand the consequences of the human impact on our planet. Liberalism is also important which is not surprising as the trait involves a readiness to challenge authority, tradition and convention. Extinction Rebellion often challenges existing social, political and economic institutions.

One faced stood out. Trust was not associated with pro-environmental attitudes and behaviours. No one should be too surprised by that. Other facets associated with green attitudes were Sympathy, Altruism, Morality Conscientiousness and Cooperation. This is again not surprising. You have to cooperate with others to achieve environmental change.

So we have an outline of the personality of the activist. She or he needs stimulation, is moral, is an achiever, has an artistic temperament and, one might add, is willing to take risks. Indulging the artistic I did warn there would be some moments when the academic tone goes off stage. Since I have written two books on Freud, I feel emboldened to conjure him up.

On the couch

The scene is Jerusalem, the holy city. Freud declined to go to Israel because his friend Stefan Zweig, one of the most-read novelists of the 1920s, told him there were no good cafes in Tel Aviv which was just a small town then. Worse the plumbing was atrocious. However, Freud now finds himself in Jerusalem in familiar surroundings because one of his devoted admirers had moved to Israel and shipped all his own furniture there. Like many Zionist analysts, he was disappointed that the local Arabs seemed to have no interest at all in being psychoanalysed.

The sign outside the house on Dizzengoff Street announces that Dr Freud will see patients by appointment only.

Trumpets sound. A golden chariot arrives at the door injuring a few pedestrians on the way. They threaten to sue the charioteer. An irascible man gets out and snaps "Just try." He then shouts;

> "Moses, I didn't give you those tablets for nothing. Do something useful. Tell Freud I'm here and I have no intention of waiting."

Moses rings the doorbell. A maid appears.

Moses: Please tell Professor Freud Professor Jehovah has arrived to see him.
Maid: Would you like some coffee, Professor?

Paula Fichtl, Freud's maid, provided his patients with coffee since she believed it would relax them before the couch ordeal.

Without answering, Professor Jehovah storms through the door to Freud's study.

Freud: I have been expecting you.
Jehovah: Don't think you can hypnotise me.
Freud: You know I don't believe in you.
Jehovah: Then what am I doing on your couch?
Freud: A good question. As the Allmighty you should not need my help.
Jehovah: I have always prided myself on loving my children, the children of Israel.
Freud: Which has not stopped you terrorising them.
Jehovah: Didn't you beat your children when they misbehaved?
Freud: My wife wouldn't let me.
Jehovah: I always prided myself on inventing punishments. Floods – a great idea. Earthquakes – wonderful

especially if a couple is fornicating. They think the earth moved. Ha! Hailstones – they should wear helmets. Droughts – plenty of those in the Middle East. Fires, hurricanes, locusts, boils – as a doctor you must treated many of those.

Freud: I was not a dermatologist. But if the creator of worlds, the destroyer of worlds, needs my help your complex must be very complex.

Jehovah starts weeping.

Freud: I always have a handkerchief for neurotic patients.

Jehovah: This is hard to say. Do you think there might be a greater God than me?

Freud: Existential anxiety. More human than divine.

Jehovah: I didn't create all these floods and fires which are threatening the earth. Even in a place called Australia which I have never heard of. So who did it?

Freud: In Greece the gods were always jealous of each other.

Jehovah: That's how I took over. But who is doing it now?

Freud: Guess.

Jehovah: Who is doing this to my children?

Freud: They are doing it to themselves.

Chapter 4

COP OUT – The Illusion of a Future, Young People's Anxieties

The title of the chapter is a deliberate variation on Freud's *The Future of an Illusion* where he argued that prehistoric humans invented God or gods because they were desperate to control terrifying natural phenomena. The Bible offers spicy descriptions of God-given disasters. The flood was small potatoes, as it were, compared to the apocalypse of the Book of Revelations, author Professor Jehovah, of course.

"And the fifth angel sounded, and I saw a star fall from heaven unto the earth: and to him was given the key of the bottomless pit.

[2] And he opened the bottomless pit; and there arose a smoke out of the pit, as the smoke of a great furnace; and the sun and the air were darkened by reason of the smoke of the pit.

[3] And there came out of the smoke locusts upon the earth: and unto them was given power, as the scorpions of the earth have power.

The scorpions however had green credentials and were told not to hurt to the grass of the earth or any tree. By verse 17 the angels were coming.

[17] And thus I saw the horses in the vision, and them that sat on them, having breastplates of fire, and of jacinth, and brimstone: and the heads of the horses were as the heads of lions; and out of their mouths issued fire and smoke and brimstone.

As we know it does not end well at Armageddon.

In the Middle Ages, preachers often foretold the end of the world. Constant plagues added to the anxiety after the Black Death killed perhaps half the population of Europe in the 14th century. The author of *Robinson Crusoe*, Daniel Defoe, in *The Journal of the Plague Year* gave a vivid account of how the bubonic decimated England in 1665.

DOI: 10.4324/9781003165484-5

If anyone complained of being sick, people assumed it was the plague. After a few days, he recovered. During the following weeks, hundreds, if not thousands, of people died from the plague in various parts of the city. Many were buried in mass graves. Some graves were looted and the population in London was noticeably less! There was "sorrow and sadness sat upon every face." So much crying and mourning could be heard from street to street.

People were imprisoned in their own homes because someone in their household had contracted the plague, and more often than not, the plague came to households through their servants. The house would be locked from the outside, and a red cross would be painted on the door. This very action could condemn some people to death as they were trapped with others who had the virus. A watchman would then be placed in front of the house. Even so, some people managed to escape through various doors in the homes, or mobs would sometimes attack the watchman and help them escape.

In Defoe's day, there were no vaccines but the fact we now have apparently safe vaccines against COVID has still left millions all over the world refusing to be jabbed.

Vaccine anxiety

Anti Vaxxers justify refusing the vaccine on the grounds that no one knows the risks. In November 2021, they were encouraged when anxieties were raised about Molnupiravir, which Merck and Ridgeback Biotherapeutics developed from an earlier, experimental antiviral. The drug works by interfering with viral replication, littering the viral genome with so many mutations until the virus can no longer reproduce.

In October 2021, company officials announced results of a clinical trial that found giving the drug to COVID-19 patients early in the disease reduced their risk of hospitalization and death by 50%. But the fact that the drug can mutate RNA has raised fears that it could induce mutations in a patient's own genetic material, possibly causing cancer or birth defects.

In November 2021, William Haseltine, a virologist formerly at Harvard University, known for his work on HIV and the human genome project, suggests that by inducing viral mutations, molnupiravir could spur the rise of new viral variants more dangerous than today's. "You are putting a drug into circulation that is a potent mutagen at a time when we are deeply concerned about new variants," Haseltine said in a Forbes blog post. "I can't imagine doing anything more dangerous."

Patients who are prescribed antibiotics and other drugs often don't complete a prescribed medication course, a practice that can allow resistant germs to survive and spread. If COVID-19 patients feel better after a couple of days and stop taking molnupiravir, Haseltine worries viral mutants will survive and possibly spread to others. "If I were trying to create a new and more dangerous virus in humans, I would feed a subclinical dose [of molnupiravir] to people infected," he added.

Then a new COVID variant identified in a handful of European countries surfaced concerns because it changed the elegant looking coronavirus spike protein in new ways. The variant, known either as B.1.X or B.1.640, was first reported by the French paper *Le Telegramme* after it infected 24 people at a French school in Brittany.

A handful of cases were also discovered in the United Kingdom, Switzerland, Scotland and Italy. Professor Cyrille Cohen of Bar Ilan University in Israel explained that the B.1.640 variant has some unprecedented mutations. One in particular has drawn attention: the spike protein, which is what allows the virus to cling to the human cell and start the infection process, has some deletions. The question is whether this will make the virus more or less infectious.

The variant is believed to have emanated from Africa where less than 10% of the population has been vaccinated.

"This variant exemplifies that if you leave some of the world's population without access to vaccines, then the virus will continue to multiply and it will lead to more variants," Cohen said. Only 6% of the population in African states is vaccinated against COVID.

"Not giving vaccines to these countries may seem OK in the short term," Cohen said, "but in the long term, we might have new variants that are problematic that developed in unvaccinated countries."

"I don't want to frighten people," he said. "There are just a few cases of B.1.640 now and it could very well be that in a month we could all forget about this variant. But it is an example of what could happen if there isn't access to vaccines for everyone."

The lure of suicide

The Guardian also reported that the year leading up to July 2017 saw a total of 95 student deaths by suicide – which equates to one in every four days.

Earlier that summer, an article by The Tab mentioned that 11 students from Bristol University killed themselves in the last 18 months – and just over half (six) of them were males.

The epidemic suicides have led people to question Bristol University's ability to provide adequate support to students suffering from mental health issues. Very few of the deaths are being reported by the media, and parents of those who died are calling for more to be done to help students who are suffering.

In a 2017 BBC Three documentary titled "Real Stories: Student Suicide," it was revealed that "one-third of students report feeling depressed or lonely" while "nearly half of students with a mental health condition do not disclose it to their universities." Universities have a duty of care to their students and do not like to parade their failings.

Across the Atlantic there were similar problems.

A 2017 survey of 20 universities in Ontario conducted by the *Toronto Star* found that very few track the number of student suicides. Public health advocates across Canada have been pushing for better data collection around suicides to better inform prevention methods.

One reason why protest against suicide is rare may be that poets have often praised death as Keats did in his Ode to a Nightingale

> Darkling I listen; and, for many a time
> I have been half in love with easeful Death,
> Call'd him soft names in many a mused rhyme,
> To take into the air my quiet breath;
> Now more than ever seems it rich to die,
> To cease upon the midnight with no pain,

The internet now offers advice on how to kill yourself which it would be irresponsible to publish. Some case histories give no advice, however, but clearly aim at a certain poetic tone like a Canadian young woman who became obsessed with researching the tallest bridges in Toronto.

"Sometimes I would stand with my toes hanging off the edge, waiting for a compassionate shove.

Don't tell anyone you are struggling with aging unless you want to elicit a laugh or an eyeroll.

'It's just a number.'

It's just a body. It's just a life.

And I had had a good one. I had a big love. I had travelled. I had made art.

To want any more, to live any longer seemed greedy.

This is the gift of trauma – never having the ability to see ahead, build a future.

Instead, the opposite – the instinct to destroy to mirror my internal devastation.

I destroyed my home, my marriage. I destroyed friendships.

Especially the ones that told me 'When you are ready, you will fix it!'

I came close to destroying my job.

Then my childhood guru died.

The one I used to pray to kill me at eleven, thirteen.

The one to whom I used to pray that we would die at the same time.

Was his death a sign, a beacon to follow?

I wanted to kill myself when I was thirty.'

Luckily, she has not done so yet."

Molly Russell was less lucky. She died in 2017. Her father Ian says believes Instagram "helped kill my daughter."

Facebook, which owns Instagram, said graphic content which sensationalises self-harm and suicide "has no place on our platform."

Ian Russell told the BBC how after his daughter died, the family began to look at the Instagram accounts she had been following from people who were depressed, self-harming or suicidal. Her own life, her family discovered distressing material about suicide on her Instagram account

"Some of that content is shocking in that it encourages self-harm, it links self-harm to suicide, and I have no doubt that Instagram helped kill my daughter."

Facebook executive Steve Hatch responded, saying, "The first thing I'd like to say is just what a difficult story it was to read and I, like anyone, was deeply upset."

"I'm deeply sorry for how this must have been such a devastating event for their family."

When confronted with print-outs of Instagram posts showing graphic photos of self-harm, he said, "We'd have to make sure that we look at these and ensure that those are taken down if they are against our policies."

"If people are posting in order to seek help and in order to seek support from communities, the experts in this area tell us that is a valuable thing for them to do. It can help with recovery; it can help with support."

"If it's there to sensationalise and glamourise, of course it has no place on our platform, it shouldn't be on our platform. And if we need to work harder to make sure it isn't on our platform then we certainly will."

It seems to take something very particular to trigger protests. Students at the University of Toronto held one to demand better mental health services and to call out the school's inaction after reports of a third suicide on campus.

Paramedics responded to a call the night before after a student was found dead on the first floor of the Bahen Centre of Information and Technology at the university.

"This is the third suicide on campus this year, and the second to occur in this building," Joshua Grodin, a student representative from the University of Toronto Students' Union, said. In June 2018, paramedics were also called to the Bahen Centre when a student died after jumping from the eighth floor into the main foyer.

Grodin says he went to speak with the vice-provost of students shortly after this incident occurred.

"I mentioned the idea of installing safety nets in the building because we had a similar incident happened earlier this year," Grodin said. "They told me they would look into solutions."

The news of yet another suicide on campus has not garnered much attention elsewhere. Students say this is because the university goes to great lengths to keep the incidents separated and quiet.

Gemima Pickles, a second-year student, said that she was left in the dark after someone in her dorm was found dead in January of this year.

In the wake of these tragedies, students are renewing calls for comprehensive mental health services.

Sheila Rasouli, a third-year neuroscience student, says she has written a letter to senior administrators calling for 21 changes to the current mental health system at the university, including more health and wellness staff, shorter wait times and increased hours during exam periods.

"By treating each death as an isolated incident, instead of part of a wider pattern, the university relinquishes themselves from making any substantial changes. The reality is three young people died in less than a year. This isn't isolated," says Alex Forgay, a second-year student at the University of Toronto.

"There are obviously deeper issues about the flawed culture of this institution that need to be addressed, but in the meantime the school needs to give mental health services the funding they need to keep students safe."

Does what could happen to your body make you more or less anxious than what could happen to the planet?

Climate calamity

Anxieties about climate change have a very long history. In the 18th century William Blake wrote of the dark Satanic mills which turned England sooty. The Swedish physicist Svante Arrhenius surveyed the first decades of the Industrial Revolution, and realized that humans were burning coal at an unprecedented rate – "evaporating our coal mines into the air." Scientists already knew that carbon dioxide trapped solar infrared radiation that would otherwise have been reflected back to space. Arrhenius did the first calculations of the possible effects of man's stepped-up production of carbon dioxide. The average global temperature, he concluded, would rise as much as nine degrees Fahrenheit if the amount of carbon dioxide in the air doubled from its pre-industrial level. Temperatures could reach 130 degrees, the sea level would rise several metres, crops would wither in the fields. He won a Nobel Prize, but not for this work.

Under sea disaster

Then, in 1957, two scientists at the Scripps Institution of Oceanography, in California, Roger Revelle and Hans Suess, published a paper in *Tellus* on the oceans. They found that the conventional wisdom was wrong: the upper layer of the oceans, where the air and sea meet and combine would absorb less than half of the excess carbon dioxide produced by humans. "A rather small change in the amount of free carbon dioxide dissolved in seawater corresponds to a relatively large change in the pressure of carbon dioxide at which the oceans and atmosphere are at equilibrium," they wrote. That is to say, most of the carbon dioxide being pumped into the air by millions of smokestacks, furnaces and car exhausts would stay in the air, where it would gradually warm the planet. "Human beings are now carrying out a large-scale geophysical experiment of a kind that could not have happened in the past nor be repeated in the future," they concluded.

In 1989 Bill McKibben reflected on this history and wrote in *The New Yorker:*

> Our comforting sense, then, of the permanence of our natural world – our confidence that it will change gradually and imperceptibly, if at all – is the result of a subtly warped perspective. Changes in our world which can affect us can happen in our lifetime – not just changes like wars but bigger and more sweeping events. Without recognizing it, we have already stepped over the threshold of such a change. I believe that we are at the end of nature.

He added:

> When I say "nature," I mean a certain set of human ideas about the world and our place in it. But the death of these ideas begins with concrete changes in the reality around us, changes that scientists can measure. More and more frequently, these changes will clash with our perceptions, until our sense of nature as eternal and separate is finally washed away and we see all too clearly what we have done.

Apocalypse anxiety

Psychology was slow to catch up, let alone link this to Freud's death wish thesis. Finally in 2017, a report by the American Psychiatric Association described apocalypse anxiety as feelings of loss, helplessness and frustration caused by "watching the slow and seemingly irrevocable impacts of climate change unfold, and worrying about the future." Neither eco-anxiety nor apocalypse anxiety has been recognised as a medical condition in the Diagnostic and Statistical Manual of Mental Disorders. But what it feels like is waking up in the middle of the night unable to breathe. The overwhelming sense is helplessness. Climate change is a steamroller – and there is not enough political will to stop it. Some common sense psychology; If something is making you anxious and powerful forces tell you to calm down, it may well make you even more anxious and succumb to fears of conspiracy.

Big Oil and big Gas had more representatives at COP26 than most countries, which fuelled fears of conspiracy. In 2018, a proposal by Royal Dutch Shell was billed as a pathway to two degrees Celsius, but it would keep similar levels of fossil-fuel production for decades. The scenario depended on carbon removal deployed on an immense scale – orders of magnitude above our current capabilities, and with potentially dangerous implications for food, energy and water security. In 2021, Shell was rebuked by a Dutch court, which ordered the company to reduce its carbon emissions by 45% by 2030.

The bottom line is usually a good motivator. Giant corporations such as Chevron and Exxon have been attacked for their inaction on the climate crisis not just by Greenpeace supporters, but by their own shareholders, who do not want their investments, excuse, to go up in smoke. China, India, Russia and Saudi Arabia have a history of minimising the problem. No one knows how much these countries spend lobbying that extracting oil is good for you.

In "White Skin, Black Fuel" (Verso), Andreas Malm and the Zetkin Collective of Scandinavia show how arguments about economic rationality get woven together with hierarchical structures and the pursuit of domination. They call this fossil fascism. In particular, its authors are struck by how the European far right has used the "funnel issue" of hostility towards immigration to promote hostility toward renewable energy.

Amitrav Ghosh, the Indian essayist, thinks that this explanation is incomplete. He wants us to reckon with broader structures of power, involving "the physical subjugation of people and territory," and, crucially, the "idea of conquest, as a process of extraction."

It sometimes sounds like a close-run race between the human race dying as a result of climate change or of COVID.

These ideas are the background to today's protests.

Extinction Rebellion

Politicians have dithered about climate change for 30 years. So now they have to deal with protest in democratic countries at least. They sometimes make good street theatre and young people often star. Extinction Rebellion started when more than 1,000 people met in Parliament Square on 31 October, 2018 to hear the "Declaration of Rebellion." They occupied the road in front of the Houses of Parliament, blockaded the UK's *Department for Business, Energy and Industrial Strategy* and unveiled a banner over *Westminster Bridge*. Cue special effects. They also glued themselves to the gates of *Downing Street* and closed an access road to *Trafalgar Square*. They also blocked the five main bridges over the *River Thames* in London for several hours – *The Guardian* described it as "one of the biggest acts of peaceful civil disobedience in the UK in decades." On "Rebellion Day 2," they staged a mock funeral march and walked to Downing Street and Buckingham Palace. The latter seems unfair now as the Queen has been caught on camera complaining politicians talk but do too little, 15 October 2021.

In June 2019, 1,000 healthcare professionals in the United Kingdom called for widespread non-violent civil disobedience in response to "woefully inadequate" government policies on the unfolding ecological emergency. They supported the school strike movement and Extinction Rebellion.

The founders of Extinction Rebellion researched the histories of "the suffragettes, the Indian salt marchers, the U.S civil rights movement and the Polish and East German democracy movements." Roger Hallam, one of the co-founders, had been an organic farmer, and has said "letters, emailing, marches don't work. You need about 400 people to go to prison. About two to three thousand people to be arrested."

A youth wing – XR Youth – of Extinction Rebellion was formed in February 2019. By October there were 55 XR Youth groups in the United Kingdom and another 25 elsewhere. To join XR Youth you have to have been born after 1990; some members are as young as ten.

In what they called the Summer Uprising of July 2019, members of XR Youth from across the South West occupied College Green and were joined by the singer Billy Bragg. Using the wall of King's College as a stage, the youth strikers set up shop and proceeded to issue damning verdicts on the state of play in the battle to put the climate emergency first and foremost on the political, cultural and financial agenda.

Having marched from Shire Hall at 10 am, around 600 protesters arrived at King's Parade in full fettle. Organisers Cambridge Schools Eco Council opened the talks

And the not even teenage compere Nico Roman, 11, introduced Billy Bragg who said, "What a powerful march that was, I liked the cowbell [this was pictured in gallery], that was really impressive, whoever is on that."

From 16 to 23 February 2020, XR Youth Cambridge held a week-long roadblock at the roundabout on Trumpington Road. They demanded The University of Cambridge cut ties with the fossil-fuel industry and Cambridge City Council hold a Citizens' Assembly on Climate Justice. Coal had to become taboo.

On Friday 21 February 2020, members of XR Youth Cambridge set up a blockade of a Shell petrol station on Newnham Road to protest the so-called greenwashing by the company. The activists held up a large banner displaying the message "Life or Death." Several climbed-on top of the station's forecourt canopy; one poured molasses onto the Shell logo from the roof making it look coated in oil.

It wasn't just the poms as the Aussies would say. On Friday 26 March 2021, members of Extinction Rebellion Youth Melbourne blocked the West Gate Freeway. They displayed a sign reading "We refuse to be the last generation." A 17-year-old from Frankston was charged with obstructing a roadway. He Instagrammed: "When injustice is law, we have a responsibility to rebel against those unjust laws, to show our dissent to a broken system." On Saturday 10 April 2021, members took part in a national day of action "to stop black deaths in custody."

There were also actions in Brazil where in 2019 Extinction Rebellion, Youth held a "public class" in Manaus to share information about the climate crisis. They displayed signs reading "NÃO HÁ PLANETA B!" ("No Planet B!") and "EMERGÊNCA CLIMÁTICA" ("Climate Emergency").

During XR's most recent actions in London, journalists would often ask protesters: aren't these tactics going to alienate people, aren't you going to lose the argument with the public? It was clear that they were quite willing to do that. Critics sniped the green policies of these middle-class deodorant-dodgers were quite prepared to make working people's lives harder and more expensive.

Prince Charles said he understood the frustration young people feel, but worried that the protest methods might alienate many people.

COP26 November 2021

As the COP26 United Nations global climate talks began in Glasgow, the *Washington Post* analysed emissions data proffered by the 197 countries at the summit, and found that they were in many cases wildly wrong. Malaysia, for instance, claimed that its forests were sucking up so much carbon that its net emissions were smaller than tiny Belgium's – even though most researchers are convinced that clearing peatlands for palm-oil plantations, as Malaysia has been doing, is the very definition of a carbon bomb. The Central African Republic reported that its land absorbs 1.8 billion tons of carbon a year; the *Post* sniped it was "an immense and improbable amount that would effectively offset the annual emissions of Russia." The emissions data could be off by 23% overall, or roughly the equivalent of China's emissions.

Meanwhile, the host government of the United Kingdom initially claimed that 190 nations represented there had joined in a breakthrough pledge to phase out coal and stop investing in new coal-power projects. Alok Sharma, who presided over the meeting did manage to get the nations to agree on many points, was rightly praised. He also cried at the end because in the final agreement India and China insisted on the phrase "phasing out coal" being replaced by "phasing down coal." Quite what that means we will discover in the future.

There were few out and out sceptics at COP26, but some clever and distinguished people remained doubtful of the orthodoxy. Nigel Lawson, the former Chancellor of the Exchequer, wrote in *The Spectator* on 6 November 2021, that in his long life "I have never come across anything remotely as bad as the current climate scare." He admitted the earth is warming "but ay a rate of at most one sixth of a degree per decade a barely perceptible amount." He then savaged the carbon dioxide thesis arguing that the main effect of carbon dioxide "in the atmosphere is to stimulate plant growth." The economic effects of decarbonisation would be catastrophic and utterly unnecessary. *The Spectator* also ran a piece called No Choice, the urgent case for net zero.

When there is no consensus, there is anxiety especially perhaps in young people whose brains are, as we have seen, more liable to emotional responses.

Chapter 5

"And That's Not Right!" Children's Sense of Justice

Jean Piaget was the most influential child psychologist of the 20th century. When he died in 1980, there were obituaries in *The Guardian* and *Le Monde* which recognised his contribution to the study of children's cognitive development. It should be said that Piaget relied a good deal on the observations his wife Valerie Chateney made.

One of Piaget's books, however, *The Moral Judgment of the Child,* was a little different though it used the same method he always did; he talked to children to find out what they believed. In that book, he studied what children found fair and unfair. Just as children's thinking changed as they grew older their ideas regarding rules, moral judgements and punishment also changed.

Piaget argued, "The child begins by simply practising reciprocity, in itself not so easy a thing as one might think. Then, once he has grown accustomed to this form of behaviour, his behaviour is altered from within, its form reacting, as it were upon its content. What is regarded as just is no longer merely reciprocal action, but primarily behaviour that admits of infinitively sustained reciprocity. The motto 'Do unto others as you would be done by' thus comes to replace the conception of crude equality" (1932, p. 404).

Piaget stressed there were two levels of morality in his native Switzerland. There was, first, a fiery Calvinist morality based on the Ten Commandments. Thou shalt *not* pre-dominated there. Authority had to be obeyed. Children were brought up in an atmosphere in which these commandments ruled, and were not up for debate. This was, Piaget argued, a primitive phase of moral thinking. He much preferred the second level of co-operative morals. Edicts from on high

DOI: 10.4324/9781003165484-6

are irrelevant. Moral co-operation is good for social life – and, perhaps, is also at the heart of a rich social life. The child understands that she has to live with others. That requires her or him to see things from others' points of view. Their intentions, desires, motives have to be taken into account. In this blessed state of unegocentric social maturity, the child comes to see that rules – and even formal laws – are only conventions. Groups can change them.

Piaget argued that moral thinking was as important as any other facet of life. He noted: "Logic is a morality of thinking just as morality is a logic of action." (1932)

Commentators usually find Piaget's work on morality a side issue. For example, the May 1982 issue of *The British Journal of Psychology,* specially devoted to Piaget, devoted only one article of five pages to it. In my *Piaget Critique and Reassessment (1982)* I argued, however, that *Moral Judgment* is central to understanding the appeal of Piaget to psychology especially as he set himself the goal of reconciling science and religious values.

Piaget (1932) suggested there were two main types of moral thinking:

1 *Heteronomous morality* which he also called moral realism.
2 *Autonomous morality* which he also called moral relativism.

Heteronomous morality is morality imposed from the outside. At first children think of morality as obeying other people's rules and laws, which cannot be changed. There were absolutes. What their parents said was wrong was. The guilty should be punished and the severity of the punishment should be related to severity of the wrongdoing. During this stage children consider rules as being unchanging and "divine like."

When they make judgements, adults usually consider motives as well as consequences, but Piaget found that for children behaviour was judged as "bad" in terms of its consequences. Intentions were irrelevant. If you break fifteen plates by accident that is worse than breaking one plate deliberately.

Young children were also unforgiving. First, they saw the function of punishment as making the guilty suffer. Punishment was an act of retribution or revenge, a deterrent to further wrongdoing. Collective punishment was seen as acceptable. Young children would accept a whole class being punished for the misdeeds of a single child.

Piaget identified a change at about the age of seven. He told children stories that embodied a moral theme and then asked for their opinion. Here are two examples:

> There was once a little girl who was called Marie. She wanted to give her mother a nice surprise and cut out a piece of sewing for her. But she did not know how to use the scissors properly and cut a big hole in her dress.

and

> A little girl called Margaret went and took her mother's scissors one day when her mother was out. She played with them for a bit. Then, as she did not know how to use them properly, she made a little hole in her dress.

Typically, younger children up to age 9–10 years of age, said that Marie is naughtier than Margaret, even though she did not mean any harm for the simple reason that the hole Marie made was bigger.

However, as children get older their attitudes change. He spent much time watching how children played marbles.

The rules of marbles

Piaget noted:

> In the first place, let us remind the reader that the behaviour of children of 3 to 7 with regard to the game of marbles is comparable on all points to the behaviour of children of the same age in regard to their conversations or to their social life or intellectual life in general. (1932, p. 69)

Piaget used the game to illustrate a child's passage through various phases before arriving at a mature, fully moral understanding of social conventions. Initially, a child plays with the marbles as interesting objects but engages in no game per se. By about age four, a child plays the game, knows how to make the right moves physically and understands the necessity for taking turns. "The child's chief interest is no longer psycho-motor; it is social," Piaget wrote.

Watching children play marbles, Piaget said, we first see the refinement of manual dexterity. And we can also observe the development of social intelligence or MI in the gamesmanship of children as they play marbles. Children deploy such gamesmanship, for example, when they manipulate the rules of the game and bluff each other to enhance the quality of play and their own success. Gamesmanship is also evident in their development of social understanding, of an appreciation of rules as rules.

"Children's games," Piaget wrote, "constitute the most admirable social institutions. The game of marbles, for instance ... contains an extremely complex system of rules, that is to say, a code of laws, a jurisprudence of its own." Piaget then began to probe the players' cognitive representation of the rules. "You begin," he said, "by asking the child if he could invent a new rule. Once the new rule has been formulated, you ask the child whether it could give rise to a new game .... The child either agrees to the suggestion or disputes it. If he agrees, you immediately ask him whether the new rule is a 'fair' rule, a 'real' rule, one 'like the others,' and try to get at the various motives that enter into the answers."

Piaget teased out distinct age-dependent styles in children's approaches to marbles.

By the age of 11, a child can explain every rule and every exception but does not yet grasp rules as rules. A child still sees them as immutable. By the age of 13, children understand that the rules are arbitrary and conventional.

People make rules and people can change them – they are not inscribed on tablets of stone. With regard to the "rules of the game" older children recognise that rules are needed to prevent quarrelling and to ensure fair play.

When children reach nine or ten, the emphasis now moves from retribution to restitution. Its purpose is not primarily to make the guilty suffer but to put things right. Punishment should also aim to get the offender to understand the harm (s)he has caused so that (s) he will not be motivated to repeat the offence. Wherever possible, punishment should fit the crime – so vandal is required to make good the damage (s)he has caused.

Older children also recognise that justice in real life is an imperfect system. Sometimes the guilty get away with their crimes and sometimes the innocent suffer unfairly. Older children nearly always consider it wrong to punish the innocent for the misdeeds of the guilty.

The ways children change is partly the result of their general cognitive development, partly due to declining egocentrism and partly due to the growing importance of peer pressure.

Piaget also argued that children then became fervent devotees of equality. Whatever the circumstances, all must be treated the same. If two children both steal sweets, their fate (dire or not) must be identical. There should be no exceptions.

This passion for equal treatment clashed rather with a previous observation Piaget made. He found that, "just at eight years, children abandoned their moral realism," which judged the gravity of a crime only in terms of its consequences and realised the importance of intentions. They no longer equated the beggar who stole bread with the spoilt brat who nicked four packets of sweets as a dare because the shopkeeper wasn't looking. Only around the age of 11 did children become more discriminating and now ethical experts, able to forgive the beggar and damn the spoilt brat. For a while, the children were miniature idealistic Marxists, judging that everyone should share what they had, and take what they need.

The story Piaget told of the picnic offered a telling example. A 7-year-old blamed the small child for being careless; he should go without cake. A 13-year-old girl was more compassionate; the culprit was very young, after all: the other children should share their food with him. Piaget saw in the difference between these two answers a wealth of moral progress.

In these egocentricity reigns, and Piaget added, "Generally speaking, one can say that motor intelligence contains the germs of completed reason. But it gives the promise of more than reason, pure and simple" (Ibid., p. 71)

In setting out such claims, Piaget was harking back to *Judgment and Reasoning in The Child,* in which he noted that advances in logic are connected with the diminution of egocentrism at the age of 7 to 8." This inability to communicate and think logically, Piaget argued, determined the rest of the child's behaviour:

> Piaget described Case 94 as he labelled it. Two little shepherd boys in the Valais were cutting hazel branches in a Y shape to represent cows. The two tips of the Y were the horns. Rules came in when the two cows fought each other. They had to stand horn to horn, and the players pushed them by pushing the base of the Y. The cow that fell on its back lost. These

> conditions had to be observed, the players had to push without jerking and the losing cow became the property of the winner.

(An aside. Switzerland runs an annual competition to find the brightest cow in the land. No other country seems as interested in cow IQ.)

Well aware that he was carrying out pioneer work, Piaget never suggested that his conclusions should be taken as definitive. He conceded that some of what he was observing might be specifically Swiss, the product of a Calvinist culture. Other cultures might inspire different moral ideas. Having made that cautious cross-cultural point, a point denied when it came to intellectual stages, Piaget went on to argue that there was a parallel between cognitive development and moral development. The weak case is that the two are merely parallel; the strong case suggests that intellectual development drives moral development.

Such failure showed that the moral realism of small children corresponded to the cognitive realism of the pre-operational child. He is ruled by immediate perceptions. Fifteen broken cups are more than one broken cup, so breaking fifteen must be more culpable. Piaget compares this rigidity to that of the child who, faced with two containers A and B, declares there is more in B, the longer one, appearances in their crudest, unanalysed forms are the only things that exist, the only sensations that can be judged. Piaget suggested that his findings about attitudes to rules revealed a similar rigidity. Before eight, children think the rules are divine, eternal and unchangeable. With lies, a similar rigidity exists. Before eight, the motive behind the lie does not matter. How much of a lie it is, however, does matter, and determines the extent of the offence? Piaget saw the moral evolution of children as an evolution, first from a state of no rules to such rigidity and then to an understanding of rules and their limits.

Heinz – whose wife had cancer

Later scholars looked at the ways Piaget's work needed improvement. Lawrence Kohlberg (1958) agreed with Piaget in principle but wanted to develop his ideas further. Like Piaget he told people stories involving moral dilemmas. One of the best-known features Heinz whose wife was dying from cancer. Doctors said a new drug might save her. It had been discovered by a local chemist, and the

Heinz tried desperately to buy some, but the chemist was charging ten times the money it cost to make the drug. Heinz could not afford it. He could raise half the money and explained to the chemist that his wife was dying. He asked if he could have the drug cheaper or pay the rest of the money later.

The chemist was an implacable capitalist. He had discovered the drug and was going to profit. Heinz was desperate so later that night he broke into the chemist's and stole the drug.

Kohlberg asked his subjects if Heinz was right to steal the drug and if it would change anything if Heinz did not love his wife or if the sufferer had been a stranger and finally if the police should arrest the chemist if Heinz's wife died. He interviewed 72 Chicago boys aged 10–16 years, 58 of whom were followed up at three-yearly intervals for 20 years (Kohlberg, 1984).

Each boy was given a two-hour interview. What Kohlberg was mainly interested in was not whether the boys judged the action right or wrong, but the reasons given for the decision. He found that these reasons tended to change as the children got older. The highest level was post-conventional morality which is characterized by an individuals' understanding of universal ethical principles. These are abstract and not always well defined but might include the preservation of life at all costs, and the importance of human dignity.

Individual judgement is based on self-chosen principles, and moral reasoning is based on individual rights and justice, according to Kohlberg. This level of moral reasoning is as far as most people get. Only 10–15% are capable of the kind of abstract thinking necessary for stage 5 or 6 where they are willing to act to defend principles like justice and equality even if it means going against the rest of society.

Most of the dilemmas are unfamiliar to most people. For example, it is all very well in the Heinz dilemma asking whether Heinz should steal the drug to save his wife. However, Kohlberg's subjects were aged between 10 and 16. They have never been married, and never been placed in a situation remotely like the one in the story. How should they know whether Heinz should steal the drug?

According to Carol Gilligan (1977), Kohlberg's theory was based on an all-male sample, and reflected a male definition of morality (it's androcentric). Men's morality is based on abstract principles of law and justice, she argued, while women's is based on principles of compassion and care which is as important.

Girls are often found to be at stage 3 in Kohlberg's system (good boy-nice girl orientation), whereas boys are more often found to be at stage 4 (Law and Order orientation). Gilligan replies:

"The very traits that have traditionally defined the goodness of women, their care for and sensitivity to the needs of others, are those that mark them out as deficient in moral development."

Gilligan stated that Kohlberg's scale systematically discriminated against women by generally placing them lower on his morality scale. She gave some anecdotal accounts of the differences between a girl (Amy) and a boy (Jake), both aged 11, in their approaches to the Heinz dilemma. Fascinated by the power of logic [Jake] locates truth in mathematics, which he says, "is the only thing that is totally logical." Considering the moral dilemma to be "sort of like a math problem with humans," he sets up an equation and proceeds to work out the solution. Jake tries to weigh the value of a life and contrasts this with the money the druggist would make from the sale. Amy's account is more equivocal and would score lower on Kohlberg's scale. Yet it is thoughtful, and it also reflects the morality of care. Asked whether Heinz should steal the drug she replied, "Well, I don't think so. I think there might be other ways besides stealing it, like if he could borrow the money or make a loan or something, but he really shouldn't steal the drug – but his wife shouldn't die either." Amy and Jake did not fit stereotypical girl-boy moulds either: Amy wanted to be a scientist, Jake an English teacher.

Further studies have, on the whole, failed to confirm her ideas. Still, Gilligan's notions of the morality of care versus the morality of justice may retain their cogency, and perhaps they do suggest that Kohlberg may have overlooked an important source of moral reasoning by neglecting the ethos of care; or at least by giving it less weight than justice in his hierarchy. Perhaps the real truth is that some boys and men do embrace a morality of care and concern; and likewise, some women and girls are more logical and less sociable in their worldviews. Is one point of view concerning moral judgements more advanced or civilized than the other? Are there two separate "tracts" or dimensions to moral reasoning? These are questions worth pondering for themselves and since they affect politics.

A personal note

I was invited to give a talk in 1996 at a conference to celebrate the centenary of Piaget's birth. I had the honour of meeting his son Laurent. Piaget based his ideas on his observations of Laurent and his sisters. I also found out that Piaget did not just study Freud but toyed with becoming a psychoanalyst and did something extraordinary; he began psychoanalysing his mother. She became increasingly annoyed with him and after a few months stopped being her son's patient. That offers an introduction to the subject of family politics.

Chapter 6

Children, Family and Politics

For every boy and every gal
Whose born into this world alive
Is either a little Liberal
Or else a little conservative
W.S Gilbert's famous lyric assumed that children would follow their parents in their political attitudes. That is less true today.

No one has to get involved with politics. Young people have more pressing stuff, getting educated, tangling with their parents and dipping their toes, as it were into sex. Sex had fewer issues in the all too macho past. My glamorous cousin Rita, who worked for Otto Preminger on *Exodus* and had an affair with a Hollywood star, gave me a book called *the Art of Dating* when I was 13. It did not ask if the reader was straight, gay, bisexual or trans. Today you could not write such a naïve book when teenagers have to struggle with their own identity.

When my cousin gave me that book, computers were so huge they often filled rooms and were only used by big business and the military. The dramatic change came at the start of the 1980s with the introduction of the personal computer. In 1982, I was a producer on an ITV show the Real World and we were given six early personal computers to see how people would use them. The families used them avidly, we learned. We were detached observers and amazed at how eager the children were to use the computers which, of course, were primitive by today's standards.

The way in which the media treated children was simple. On shows like Blue Peter they were shown how to do things mainly. It has become very different now.

DOI: 10.4324/9781003165484-7

Children on the media

On 25 October 2021, an edition of the Channel 4 strand Dispatches gave a good example of letting children have their say. It followed four 9-year-old boys who were in danger of becoming homeless. They were constantly worried about money, aware that if they did not find the rent they would be evicted. Their interviews were articulate and poignant. For them childhood was not a time of innocence but of fear. Al Jazeera runs a regular strand which gives young people a chance to speak. On 26 October, three were sharp in suggesting the old people who run the world would be dead by the time of the worst disasters. Then Sky TV runs a News Club which tells young viewers:

> "If you love investigating fake news and the world around us then here's some good news ... we have launched the FYI News Club for schools. We will provide everything you need for you and your teachers to help you get it going. It's a great way to get together, watch FYI with your mates and investigate fake news, and find more info about the big stories."

FYI also hosts Junior Prime Minister's Questions, "where you get to ask the country's leader your very own questions! You can send us your questions below, and we'll contact your parent or carer if we'd like to shortlist yours."

At the opening of COP26, UK television channels gave children an unprecedented chance to express their fears. ITV London news listened in to a primary class in a Greenwich school. The children were aware of the risks of rising temperatures and were very divided about the capacity of politicians to solve the problems. Prince Charles warned that the planet had little time to find solutions while outside his son Prince William and his wife talked to children about the perils. One boy worried that when global warming made the earth impossibly hot it would not be possible to decamp to Mars because that planet would not be welcoming.

All these opportunities prompt the question.

How much do young people know?

One of the questions old people who may be dementing are asked is who is the Prime Minister or the President? I have tried to find research on how much eight- and ten-year-olds children know about politics. There seems to be none.

In general, the drawback of much research until very recently is that the subjects tended to be white American undergraduates. It seems to me there are three key questions:

How much time do children spend on political activity?
How involved are they with political organisations?
How much do they know about political issues?

A 2016 survey by the Annenberg Public Policy Centre found that only 26% of Americans could name all three branches of government, far less than earlier. Public trust in government is at only 18% and voter participation has reached its lowest point since 1996. The survey warned that without an understanding of the structure of government, our rights and responsibilities, voter apathy will continue to plague American democracy. Teachers and schools had to make sure that young people become engaged and knowledgeable citizens.

America requires high school students to pass the US citizenship exam before graduation. Yet, critics argue that the citizenship test does nothing to measure how well students understand the material. They argue this is a shame as when civics education is taught well, it can equip students with the knowledge and skills they need.

In a study by the Joseph Rowntree foundation, a team of researchers at the University of Kansas sought to learn more about the political development of American children. In 2016 Hillary Clinton was the first woman to stand for the presidency for a major party so the researchers also examined children's knowledge of gender and politics. Broadly children were interested in and had some knowledge about the election and candidates, but many had gaps in their knowledge.

"Our research argues for the establishment of a developmental science of politics that describes and predicts the formation and change of individuals' political knowledge, attitudes, and behaviour beginning in childhood and continuing across the life course," said Dr Meagan Patterson, Associate Professor at the University of Kansas' School of Education.

Over 90% of the children could provide information about at least one of the candidates. Nearly all expressed a preference for one candidate and knew the election outcome. Eighty per cent made at least one reference to a candidate's *personal characteristics* (such as being smart, nice, mean or rude). Children were equally likely to mention positives and negatives, but more children mentioned positive characteristics for Clinton than for Trump. Most children in the sample were drawn from areas in which most voters supported Clinton and that may explain these findings.

Children were more likely to support Trump when they reported that their parents supported Trump. Children, however, generally knew little about women's underrepresentation in government. Nearly half of the children sampled reported that 50% or more of all US governors and members of Congress are women, whereas the accurate percentages at that time were around 20%. Only 65% of children knew that no woman has ever been president of the United States, a smaller percentage than has been found in past studies.

"Although our study focused on the 2016 United States *presidential election* in particular, the data emphasize the need for high quality civics education throughout childhood more generally," according to Dr Rebecca Bigler, Professor Emeritx at the University of Texas at Austin. "Additionally, children should be given opportunities to take *knowledge* and views outside the walls of their own classroom and apply them to larger communities (their schools, neighbourhoods, cities." That would foster their interest and political efficacy.

How much do they care?

A number of surveys suggest that even if the young do not vote they care passionately about some issues. One survey of 16–24-year-olds showed that 20% had volunteered for a charity in the past year. Rather more had signed an online petition 53%.

Forty-five per cent supported peaceful protests (such as Extinction Rebellion's "shut down London"). Fifty-four per cent believed that protest marches achieve their purpose more often than not.

The survey found that the top political issues worrying young UK adults (aged 18–24) are the cost of living, finding housing they can afford, unemployment, the future of the NHS, inequality, university fees, the state of UK public finances (and that before COVID-19 forced the government to spend more than ever before), care for the elderly, levels of crime and access to welfare.

Politicians need to sit up and take notice

Anyone who thinks that young voters can't influence politicians is massively mistaken.

Hansard's 2019 Audit of Political Engagement found that 47% of 18–24-year-olds are certain to vote, compared to just 39% in 2016. This could suggest that the time has come for politicians to sit up and take notice of young adults finally.

There have been changes in the youth vote between 2017 and now. The Conservatives have lost 14% of their 2017 voters aged 18–29 to the Lib Dems, and another 6% to Labour.

As well as more children being on the media, there are institutions worth noting.

School councils

A school council to which children are usually elected by their classmates offers way in which pupils can voice their opinions and have their views taken into account in decisions. A selection of those schools demonstrating good practice in this regard have been identified by the Education and Training Inspectorate (ETI).

Schools will also be able to access best practice material on Every School a Good School TV in due course.

Children's parliaments

One of the first children's parliaments had an unlikely origin. It was set up in the 1990s in village schools in Rajasthan, India, which involves children aged six to fourteen electing child representatives who have been able to make genuine differences for their communities. Some children's parliaments, such as in the city of Barra Mansa in Brazil, have extensive powers over children's issues and control parts of the government budget.

Scotland has a Youth Parliament which is democratically elected. Usefully its website and social media channels are updated every day with the latest information for young people on COVID-19. It also co-produced Lockdown Lowdown – a survey of young people on their concerns about COVID-19. The survey received 2,419 responses from young people aged 11–25 across Scotland.

Forty-two per cent stated that they were Extremely or Moderately concerned about school, college and university closures. Forty-nine per cent said that they were Moderately or Extremely concerned about exam grades. Sixty-one per cent stated that they were Moderately or Extremely concerned about the impact of coronavirus on their future. Politicians seem to have failed. The majority of respondents (87%) stated that politicians should be providing information around coronavirus

Respondents were asked to provide examples of actions that they would like to see decision-makers take to tackle issues surrounding coronavirus, 10% of respondents noted they wanted to see improvements to the current impact on education.

Subjects were worried about estimated grades (instead of completing coursework or exams this year)? Estimated grades might penalise pupils who may have performed better in exams and this could damage young people's future education and employment opportunities. These examples of listening to children need to be seen in the context of research.

You are a dummy dad – and you're no better mum!

One of the questions all this raises is the influence of parents.

We now come to a paradox or perhaps a change due to technology. T.E. Erika Patterson wrote in an article in the Atlantic in May 2014 that many parents try to teach their children and impart their views, perhaps hoping their children would become carbon copies of themselves or become the people they wish they were themselves. Some parents try to indoctrinate their children raising them to be young ideologues. But new research suggests trying to plant those seeds during potty training might actually be the fastest way to guarantee political rebellion later on. A. Patterson reported on a number of couples.

Jennifer and Ryan Russon of Coral Springs, Florida, are raising their son Maxwell, age eight, and daughter Anna, age six, to become staunch liberals and atheists. Their family refuses to shop at Walmart because its owners are, according to Ryan, "goose-stepping Nazis."

"Both kids already understand that the minimum wage needs to be raised," Jennifer explains. "In fact, my son had to pick a president to do a report on in his third-grade class and wrote an essay about how being able to afford food is a basic human right – that this would be his first initiative were he POTUS." POTUS is the President.

There were consequences at school. Anna annoyed her conservative kindergarten teacher when she announced that she would not eat Papa John's pizza during a class party because the company's Chief Executive was reluctant to provide healthcare benefits to his employees.

"We make sure the kids know that just because daddy may make more money than somebody else that does not mean he is a harder worker or made better choices," Jennifer explained. "Certainly this is sometimes the case, but it is not always the case. Feeling empathy and seeing the bigger picture is a big part of being liberal and I think we do a good job of impressing this on our kids."

However, all these seemingly well-meaning efforts may be in vain. Elias Dinas in a recent paper in *the British Journal of Political Science*, based on data from the United States and United Kingdom, found that parents who insist that their children adopt their political views inadvertently influence them to abandon the belief once they become adults. The mechanism is perhaps surprising: children who come from homes where politics is a frequent topic of discussion are more likely to talk about politics once they leave home, exposing them to new viewpoints – which they then adopt with surprising frequency.

The study also showed that these changes are especially likely to happen during the college years. Conservative culture warriors have warned for years that universities are outposts of liberal indoctrination – and the study seems to confirm at least some of that warning.

"Extreme parental views of the world give children a clear choice for being with the parents through agreement, or against parents through disagreement," according to Carl Pickhardt, an author and child psychologist. "Thus extremely rigid views of right/wrong, trust/distrust, love/hate can be embraced by children who want to stay connected to parents, and can be cast off by children who, for their own independence, are willing to place the parental relationship at risk."

The Dinas study shows how quickly that teaching can be set aside when children start to think for themselves.

Chapter 7

Technoference: Or How Technology Warps the Bonds between Parents and Children

In 1944, the English psychoanalyst John Bowlby published a now-classic paper on 44 juvenile thieves. They had become delinquent, Bowlby argued, because they had not had a steady presence – in those days it was a mother's presence – and source of love, Bowlby told me in an interview with the New Scientist. Love requires attention – and technology makes it harder to give that as the screen that takes precedence all too often.

More than a quarter of American adults now report that they are online "almost constantly," according to a Pew Research Center survey. Psychologists worry about potentially *devastating consequences* for the development of babies and toddlers.

"The most important thing for little people in the zero-to-three range is interactions with human beings," according to Kathy Hirsh-Pasek, a senior fellow at the Brookings Institution. "Anything that disrupts the timing, or the meaningfulness, or the emotional quality of that interaction can have consequences on both parents and kids and on their relationship." Hirsh-Pasek says "I don't care if you're in Mongolia, or China, or the United States or Great Britain," she says. "Kids grow up the same way. They need human interaction."

Brandon McDaniel, an Indiana-based researcher on family relationships, has coined a word to describe this phenomenon: "*technoference.*" Some have even likened it to an addiction and like all addiction it rots relationships. Basically, our phones have become a permanent extension of our hands, and we don't pay much attention to the actual world around us. We have substituted virtual reality for reality, and it turns out that switching back and forth between the two worlds doesn't come so easily.

DOI: 10.4324/9781003165484-8

A study published in the journal *Psychology of Popular Media Culture,* researchers found that 70% of women said that smartphones interfered with their relationship. In *The Devil Wears Prada,* the heroine always takes calls from her boss played by Meryl Streep at her most imperious. The heroine's exasperated boyfriend tells her the person whose calls you always take is your significant other. In the end heroine tosses her phone into a fountain during Paris fashion week.

It is rude to stare at your phone while your partner is talking to you, because this tells them that what they have to say doesn't matter. The same study that found 70% of women had "technoference" in their relationships also discovered that *62% of women said technology interfered with leisure time with their partner.*

This creates dissatisfaction and loneliness in a relationship especially if your partner keeps on choosing the phone or screen over you. The whole point of a relationship is to have someone to talk to and bond with? A small device that gives us a gateway to a virtual world can literally cause someone we love in the real world to fade away.

This is not the only way the use of technology causes depression. The blue light emitted from smartphones can interrupt our circadian rhythm, leading to sleep problems, which can result in a depressed mood.

In 2015, security software company AVG Technologies surveyed 6,000 families with kids between 8and 13 years old in ten countries, including Brazil, Czech Republic and New Zealand, about their tech use. Over half of children said their parents checked their devices too often. More than half of the parents agreed. Meanwhile, 32% of kids reported feeling "unimportant" when parents checked their phones.

Technology, however, can be an incredibly helpful tool for families. Online forums can provide support for overwhelmed parents, and high-quality educational apps can help structure children's learning. And we don't yet know enough about the connection and long-term impact between parents' tech use and child development, says McDaniel. But experts agree that, when it comes to infants and toddlers, it's best to *avoid or severely limit screen time*. Why not limit parents' screen time as well?

Hirsh-Pasek believes limiting tech use could benefit parents as well as their babies. "There's nothing more addictive than looking into a young child's eyes, and listening to them, and learning about their world," she says. Technoference has, "in a sense, robbed us from having those kinds of rich experiences that bond parents and children." Both suffer, especially as children have more expertise than their parents.

And they start young. On the London Overground, I get into conversation with a man whose boy is playing with a tablet. I explain I am writing a book and ask how good the boy is with the tablet. "Good," the man replies. "My two-year-old daughter is also not bad on it." At that age Einstein had not uttered a word.

A recent paper published in *the Journal of Communication* found that between 30% and 40% of parents were taught how to use the computer and internet by their children. In most cases, parents have no idea that they are being influenced by their children. This is especially true in lower socio-economic families. It's thought that this happens because children learn, and are influenced by, their peers. And also due to greater technology education in schools. Whereas parents spend their days working and are confined to whatever practices make up their normal working day.

In a recent *policy statement*, the American Academy of Paediatrics advised parents not to use technology as a way to calm or pacify negative emotions in their children. The Academy warned, "concern that using media as a strategy to calm could lead to problems with limit setting or the inability of children to develop their own emotion regulation."

Basically, children need the experience of feeling these emotions and practise tolerating them to develop self-control and emotional intelligence.

Chapter 8

The Paradox of Tech-savvy and IQ

In 1902 the city of Paris commissioned two French psychologists, Alfred Binet and Theodore Simon, to examine the effectiveness of schools. The city wanted to provide extra help for children who were not doing well. Binet and Simon came up with the idea of measuring *norms of achievement* for different ages.

They looked at what most children of a particular age could achieve. They soon came up with lists of tasks that a normal four-year-old child could perform. To modern psychologists, their lists are a quaint mix of tasks. Four- to six-year-old children were given a set of instructions to follow. For one task, they were told to pick up a key, put it on a chair at one end of the room, shut a door, then pick up a box and bring it back to the experimenter. To succeed the child had to remember a sequence of five actions. That was beyond most four-year-olds.

Half the five-year-olds Binet and Simon tested, however, did manage the sequence. Through such exercises the researchers established norms. The average six-year-olds could manage the following:

distinguish between morning and evening
copy the picture of a diamond
count thirteen pennies
distinguish between pictures of ugly and pretty faces.

The normal eight-year-old child could manage to:

compare two objects from memory
count to 20 without hesitation

DOI: 10.4324/9781003165484-9

say what had been left out of a picture he had just seen
repeat a list of five digits.

Binet and Simon's questions have many of the characteristics of IQ tests. Seven of the eight questions have a clear right or wrong answer; the only one where there is room for debate is what is a pretty and an ugly face. Is what a Paris psychologist thinks of as a pretty face the universally correct answer? In the South Pacific they might have different ideas. Binet and Simon's questions also don't touch the question of children's creative or imaginative thinking.

As Binet and Simon discovered what was normal for children of different ages, they were able to quantify just how clever or not a particular child was in comparison with other children. The IQ test is a comparative measure, not an absolute one. If I weigh 62 kilos that is an absolute measure. I may be light or heavy for my age and height but the 62 kilos are 62 kilos.

Binet and Simon's work led to the birth of the IQ which stands for *Intelligence Quotient*. You would give a child a series of 20 questions. The psychologist knew the norm for six-year-olds was to be able to answer 14 of these questions.

If a child got 14 out of the 20 questions right, he or she would have an IQ of 100, dead average. Simon and Binet's norms made it possible to work out what the child's mental age was. If an eight-year-old child could answer 12 questions and that was normal for an eight-year-old child, then his or her intelligence quotient was 125.

The IQ was this fraction:

Mental age/chronological age × 100.

With the six-year-old child who answered all the questions an eight-year-old child should, his IQ score would be:

8 divided by 6 = 1.25 × 100 = 125.

IQ testing was soon taken up by the American army who were interested in adults. During the 1914 war, IQ tests were used on 1.75 million recruits. The huge amount of data generated encouraged researchers to study how fair the tests were and to improve their design.

Robert Yerkes, who is best remembered for his work on apes, developed the Army Alpha test to evaluate the many US recruits during the 1914–1918 war. It was introduced to systematically evaluate the intellectual and emotional functioning of soldiers. The test measured "verbal ability, numerical ability, ability to follow directions or orders, and knowledge of information." The scores were used to determine a soldier's capability of serving, what job would suit him best and his potential for a leadership position. Soldiers who were illiterate or foreign speaking would take the Army Beta, the nonverbal equivalent of the exam. No person was reported as feeble-minded until a detailed individual psychological examination had been made. Many cases of mental disorder were discovered and referred to the psychiatrists. Both the Army Alpha and Army Beta tests were discontinued after the First World War but IQ thrived. In 1927, Spearman proposed the g factor of general intelligence which became very influential. Britain saw a major scandal when Sir Cyril Burt who was a zealot for IQ turned out to have invented results that showed intelligence was largely inherited.

IQ seemed to rise in the 1930s to 1960s which was attributed to better nutrition among other factors. Eysenck, who was unfairly pilloried as a racist, showed the IQ scores of Chinese people were higher than of whites. This rise and rise has since been dented as worldwide studies of IQ showed that children appear to be less intelligent than their parents or grandparents. Yet these are the generation that has mastered much technology.

In the 1980s, I co-wrote *Testing Psychological Tests* which scrutinised the most used of over 8,000 psychological tests. It covered the issue of whether IQ tests really measured intelligence. This is a complicated subject and there have been many critiques of IQ tests, but they are still relied on in recruitment and education though often now in combination with other tests.

Today's children have been brought up using computers and playing computer games very young, which makes comparing their skills with those of earlier generations hard.

The use of the internet shows children today know more of the world and one might imagine this would make them smarter than ever before. The research suggests differently, however. The IQ levels of young people have been steadily falling for the past few decades, according to recent research.

The decline is believed to have begun after the generation born in 1975 and indicates that the slow rise in intelligence observed over much of the 20th century has come to an end.

Average IQs had risen by roughly three percentage points every decade since the Second World War, in a poorly understood trend known as the Flynn effect after the psychologist who popularised the finding.

However, a new study, by Norwegian researchers, found that men's IQs are measurably lower today than the scores of their fathers at the same age. Ole Rogeberg and Bernt Bratsberg, of the Ragnar Frisch Centre for Economic Research in Oslo, analysed the IQ scores of more than 730,000 Norwegian men who reported for national service between 1970 and 2009. Those born in 1991 scored about five points lower than those born in 1975.

"This is the most convincing evidence yet of a reversal of the Flynn effect," according to Stuart Ritchie, a psychologist at the University of Edinburgh. "If you assume their model is correct, the results are impressive, and pretty worrying."

The reasons for the Flynn effect and its apparent reversal are disputed. Scientists have put the rise in IQ down to better teaching, nutrition, healthcare and even artificial lighting. A rival thesis is that the nature of intelligence is changing in the digital age and cannot be captured with traditional IQ tests. An international study in 2020 pointed towards the onset of technology as hindering the development of young people.

According to Michael Shayer, who co-authored a technique called cognitive acceleration, since 1995 a "large social force has been interfering with children's development of thinking, getting larger each year." This "social force" includes the development of technology, such as game consoles and smartphones, "which have altered the way that children communicate with each other," he explained.

"Take 14-year-olds in Britain. What 25% could do back in 1994, now only 5% can do," Shayer added, citing maths and science tests. We have a curious paradox here. While children perform less well on IQ tests they do know how to find out things because they are more tech-savvy.

IQ is often hailed as a crucial driver of success, particularly in science, innovation and technology but some of the greatest human achievements have relied on traits IQ does not touch. Creativity, imagination, curiosity and empathy matter. Liam Hudson explored this in his *Contrary Imaginations*. When I interviewed him in 1977, he pointed out that traditional questions in creativity tests included how many uses can you think for a match or a brick. The more answers you gave the more creative you were. When he studied school children, Hudson found that some of the most obviously creative ones had no interest in this.

He told me he had tried to follow Getzels and Jackson's work on IQ. "You know that Getzels and Jackson had contrasted high IQ and high creative children. I found that this was confounded with specialisation in the arts and sciences." He admitted it was pure luck.

Hudson died sadly young before the concept of "cognitive flexibility" was mooted. This is the capacity to switch between different concepts, or to adapt behaviour to achieve goals in a novel or changing environment. It is essentially about learning to learn and being flexible about the way one learns. It lets us see that what we are doing is not leading to success and allows us to make the appropriate changes to achieve it. If you normally take the same route to work, but roadworks now clog your usual route, what do you do? Some people remain rigid and stick to the original plan, despite the delay. More flexible people adapt to the unexpected event and work out a solution.

Cognitive flexibility is also associated with higher resilience when life becomes difficult as well as better quality of life in older individuals. Studies have shown that cognitive flexibility has a strong link to the ability to understand the emotions, thoughts and intentions of others.

The opposite of cognitive flexibility is cognitive rigidity, which is found in a number of mental health disorders including obsessive-compulsive disorder, depression and being on the autism spectrum disorder.

It is possible to train cognitive flexibility. Cognitive behavioural therapy (CBT), for example, can help people change their patterns of thought and behaviour. For example, a person with depression who has not been contacted by a friend in a week may attribute this to the friend no longer liking them. In CBT, the goal is to reconstruct their thinking to consider more flexible options, such as the friend being busy or unable to contact them.

As we come out of the pandemic, we will need to ensure that in teaching and training new skills, people also learn to be cognitively flexible. This will give them greater resilience and wellbeing.

Science fiction has for decades toyed with the idea that robots and super-smart computers will out do humans – again a cause of anxiety.

Chess and flexibility – the best human can still beat the machine just about

On 10 February 1996, after three hours, world chess champion Garry Kasparov lost the first game of a six-game match against Deep Blue, an IBM computer. It could evaluate 200 million moves per second. In the end, Kasparov beat Deep Blue in the match with three wins and two ties and took home the $400,000 prize. It was a close-run thing, however.

In 2003, Kasparov battled another computer program, "Deep Junior." The match ended in a tie. Kasparov retired from professional chess in 2005.

The chess-playing computer is one example of artificial Intelligence(AI). AI applications include advanced web search engines (i.e. Google), recommendation systems (used by YouTube, Amazon and Netflix), understanding human speech (such as Siri or Alexa), self-driving cars (e.g. Tesla), automated decision-making and competing at the highest level in games (such as chess and Go). The self-driving car is not such a triumph yet, nor is the so-called smart motorway.

AI has experienced several waves of optimism, followed by disappointment. AI research has tried and discarded many different approaches including simulating the brain, modelling human problem solving, formal logic, large databases of knowledge and imitating animal behaviour.

The field was founded on the assumption that human intelligence can be so precisely described that a machine can be made to simulate it. This raises philosophical arguments about the mind and the ethics of creating artificial beings endowed with human-like intelligence. These issues have been explored by myth, fiction and philosophy since antiquity. There are the optimists who think AI will make life easier and most humans will no longer have to work at boring jobs. The pessimists counter we better keep the robots on a leash as they may aspire to take over. Data, the android in *Star Trek*, wants to be a human but he is loyal to Captain Jean Luc Picard and never sins. The pessimists fear Data is an exception and less pliable robots may become an existential risk to humanity.

Children are often at the forefront when it comes to using and being used by AI, and that can leave them in vulnerable. "Because they are developing intellectually and emotionally and physically, they are very shapeable," according to Steve Vosloo, a policy specialist for digital connectivity at UNICEF, the United Nations Children Fund.

Vosloo led the drafting of a new set of guidelines from UNICEF designed to help governments and companies develop AI policies that consider children's needs. The guidelines are meant to consider children and insist AI systems should not just be explainable – they should be explainable to the young. "Children have additional rights to adults," Vosloo says. "We're not talking about a minority group here," he points out.

"We come into this with eyes wide open," Vosloo says. "We understand this is kind of new territory for many governments and companies. So if over time we see more examples of children being included in the AI or policy development cycle, more care around how their data is collected and analysed – if we see AI made more explainable to children or to their caregivers – that would be a win for us."

Chapter 9

Children as Victims Too

It would be impossible to write on this topic without considering the situations in which children and young people are victims of violence, sexual abuse, are made to work as slaves and forced to become soldiers. The ages at which they are made to suffer are shocking; even babies are often abused.

I have made two films about child abuse. One followed the Yorkshire Police, I saw how the police struggled with getting children to explain what had happened to them. Officers used anatomical dolls to prompt the children's memories. Nearly always children have been silent and blame themselves for what has happened to them.

In Victorian times, thousands of child prostitutes, male and female, offered themselves in every large city. Oscar Wilde certainly enjoyed "rent boys" as they were called. Freud complicated matters when he argued that many stories of abuse were wished fulfilments; it was children who wanted to be seduced by their parents. It took him years to admit that he had been wrong and that he had worried the truth – that parents are abusive – would prejudice scientists against psychoanalysis. In the 1920s and 1930s, the psychologist Carl Rogers studied young children in Rochester in New York state and found that quite a few of them had considerable sexual knowledge. He deduced they had been abused. His ideas were not well received so he left the subject behind and developed client-centred therapy.

After 1940 the subject was largely ignored in medicine and politics. When children in Britain were evacuated during the war many suffered because of the separation from their parents. It seems likely that some would have been vulnerable to abuse. There

DOI: 10.4324/9781003165484-10

is apparently no systematic study of this, and it would make an excellent thesis subject.

Today some patterns are clear. Sexual abuse often occurs in families involving most often fathers or father figures, uncles or older brothers. About half the victimization of girls occurs within the family. For boys the figure is only 10–20%. But the predators are not just in the family. Childcare workers, teachers, clergy, music teachers and sport coaches have been found guilty of preying on children.

In Britain the subject of child abuse hit the headlines with the Maria Colwell tragedy. She was the youngest of five children, whose mother then had three more in a quick succession by another man. She was known to the National Society for the Prevention of Cruelty to Children (NSPCC) and the local Children's Department and neighbours repeatedly reported her being beaten and bruised. Maria apparently got help. She was seen by an NSPCC inspector, a social worker, a doctor, an education welfare officer and a housing officer. They all failed to see the danger she was in. On 7 January 1973, she was taken to hospital in a pram by her mother and stepfather where she was pronounced dead from severe bruising and internal injuries. Her stomach was empty.

Over ten years later, Tyra Henry was allowed to live with her father when he was discharged from prison despite having assaulted her six-month-old brother so viciously that he was left blind, permanently brain damaged and in care. One weekend in 1984 her father, Andrew, beat both Tyra and her mother Claudette. Her mother went out and her father launched the final assault on 22-month-old Tyra who was then taken to hospital in a mini-cab and left under a false name. Fifty bite marks were found on her body, and she died two days later.

These were cases of violence but by 1991 when I made my second film on abuse, called *The Last Taboo*, sexual abuse was finally being studied. I interviewed a 30-year-old man who had been abused by his own father. The abuse started with his father playing with his genitals when he was bathing the boy. My interviewee started to abuse other children when he was ten. It did not seem wrong to him because of his own experiences. I reported a study which found that one-third of abusers had been victims of abuse themselves.

Another case shocked Britain in 2007. Peter Connolly, also known as "Baby P," was a 17-month-old British boy who died in

London in 2007 after suffering more than 50 injuries over an eight-month period. He was repeatedly seen by the London Borough of Haringey Children's services and National Health Service health professionals. Baby P's real first name was revealed as "Peter" at the end of a subsequent trial of Peter's mother's boyfriend on a charge of raping a two-year-old.

Baby P had lived and died in horrible conditions. Contrasting Baby P's existence with that of a child of respectable, middle-class parents, Hitchens wrote:

> But things are different in the earthly hell inhabited by Baby P. His "home" was filthy and lice ridden; it stank of piss and shit and there were smelly aggressive dogs there too.
>
> (*Mail on Sunday*, 16 November 2008)

The child protection services of Haringey and other agencies were widely criticised. Three enquiries and a nationwide review of social service care were launched, and the Head of Children's Services at Haringey was removed.

Though there was far more awareness, the issue became even more controversial when it became entangled with race. In Rochdale girls were being targeted by Pakistani men – and that the police were not inclined to pursue them for fear of being accused of racism.

Finally, nine men who abused girls as young as 13 were convicted over a child sex grooming ring, guilty of twenty-one counts of sexual abuse over a two-year period. Girls who were as young as 13 when the abuse happened between 2008 and 2010 gave evidence. Some of them had run away from home or were in the care of social services. The abusers gave them the attention they craved before getting them drunk, raping them and driving them all over the north to have sex with other men.

Maggie Oliver, one of the policewomen involved in the Rochdale investigation, told the Daily Mail in 2021:

> It's been ten years since I resigned as detective constable from Greater Manchester Police in protest at how the victims of the Rochdale grooming gang were repeatedly failed.

And so little has changed since then. This most horrific child abuse case continues to expose so much of what is wrong with our so-called justice system. Whether that are inadequate charges, pitiful sentences, lack of victim care or systemic failures in prosecutions, this case exposes the lot, and it still makes my blood boil.

We discovered in January 2022 that Adil Khan and Abdul Rauf, two convicted members of the notorious grooming gang, are fighting deportation from the United Kingdom on the grounds this will breach THEIR human rights! But what about the human rights of the victims, whose lives they destroyed?

Adil Khan was a married man of 40 with three kids when he abused multiple children over many years, including a girl of just 13 who he made pregnant. He repeatedly denied this, but a DNA test proved he was the father.

At least 47 children were groomed and abused by the gang of which Khan and Rauf formed part, but despite the magnitude of the crimes, Khan served less than four years of an eight-year sentence, Rauf just two and a half of his six-year sentence.

In a recent court appearance, Khan had the nerve to claim, "We have not committed that big a crime."

Every conceivable agency – doctors, social workers, police charities – had let these children down. In 2019, a major retrospective enquiry started in Britain. One of its reports of the Alexis Jay enquiry highlighted the complicity of religious organisations. It had examined evidence received from 38 religious organisations in England and Wales. It criticised the blatant hypocrisy of religions purporting to teach right from wrong and yet failing to prevent or respond to child sexual abuse. It gave some case histories.

PR-A10 was sexually assaulted by a church volunteer when she was 12 years old. PR-A10 disclosed the abuse to her mother, who reported it to the police. After being made aware of the allegations, a church minister told her mother that the abuser was "valued" and must be considered "innocent until proven guilty."

PR-A22, PR-A23, PR-A24 and PR-A25 were all sexually abused when they were approximately nine years old while they were being taught the Qur'an by a teacher in a mosque. In 2017, the perpetrator was convicted and sentenced to 13 years' imprisonment.

Professor Alexis Jay, Chair of the Inquiry, said: "*When we heard about shocking failures to prevent and respond to child sexual abuse across almost all major religions, it became clear many are operating in direct conflict with this mission.*"

"Blaming the victims, fears of reputational damage and discouraging external reporting are some of the barriers victims and survivors face, as well as clear indicators of religious organisations prioritising their own reputations above all else. For many, these barriers have been too difficult to overcome."

One victim, identified only as A711, said, "The church needs a seismic shift in culture, especially at the top. If there is any hope at all of real change it will require a relinquishing of power, and a will to treat survivors as human beings."

Between 1970 and 2015, the church in England and Wales received more than 900 complaints involving more than 3,000 instances of child sexual abuse, made against more than 900 individuals, including priests, monks and volunteers.

The abuse involved instances of "masturbation, oral sex, vaginal rape and anal rape." On occasions it was accompanied by "sadistic beatings driven by sexual gratification" as well as "deeply manipulative behaviour by those in positions of trust."

One child estimated that between the ages of 11 and 15 he had been abused hundreds of times by a priest. "After each incident he was required to make confession, and the priest concerned made it plain that his sister's place at a local convent school depended on his compliance," the report says.

The enquiry asked the Vatican's ambassador to the United Kingdom, the papal nuncio, to participate. "Very limited information was forthcoming," the report complains. "After several months of correspondence, the in this case not so Holy See belatedly confirmed it would not provide a witness statement." "Their lack of cooperation passes understanding."

Jay accused that, "It is clear that the church's reputation was valued above the welfare of victims, with allegations ignored and perpetrators protected. Even today, the responses of the Holy See appear at odds with the pope's promise to take action on this hugely important problem."

Accusations highlighted the role of Cardinal Nichols. Richard Scorer, a solicitor at the law firm Slater and Gordon, who represented 32 survivors, said, "Cardinal Nichols needs to resign right away – in any other walk of life he would be gone immediately. This is a church that cannot be trusted to protect children. The only way forward now is a mandatory reporting law, so that abuse cannot be covered up, and independent external oversight of church safeguarding."

One survivor represented by solicitors Slater and Gordon said, "Vincent Nichols will retire with a full pension – meanwhile, the victims that he denied justice to have to live on, still suffering."

"The fact is Nichols is a serial protector of paedophiles and he is the person that you should least expect it from. The head of a church should have the greatest morals of all but instead they were sending paedophiles to other areas of the country – and America – in an attempt to cover the abuse up."

Responding to calls for Nichols' departure, a church spokesperson said the cardinal would not be resigning following the enquiry's criticisms because he was "determined to put it right."

A statement issued by Nichols and the Archbishop of Liverpool, Malcolm McMahon, said the Catholic church welcomed the report, which would "inform" improvements in "safeguarding in all aspects of the church's life."

It added, "We apologise to all victims and survivors who have not been properly listened to, or properly supported by us."

In October 2021, the French government released a report that said 330,000 children had been abused by priests over the last 70 years. In Ireland, enquiries have singled out the Magdalena laundries where unmarried girls who had given birth were treated as slaves by the nuns.

In November 2021, the Catholic paper, *The Tablet*, reported on a book which urged an end to compulsory celibacy which it saw as an escape from women. Women should be fully integrated into the power structures of the church including investigations into abuse. Women should also be involved in choosing clergy and should take over investigations into complaints from bishops. The chance of these proposals being accepted by the Church is slim.

It is not only clergy who abuse their position.

Gymnasts and their coaches

Some cases hit the headlines because the victim is famous. The gymnast Simone Biles, who won 32 world and Olympic medals, has admitted that she should have walked away from the Olympic programme "way before" the Tokyo Games. She withdrew to focus on her mental health after suffering from a phenomenon known as the twisties that affected her spatial awareness.

Biles revealed in 2018 that she was one of the US gymnasts abused by the team doctor, Larry Nassar. When testifying at a senate committee hearing into the FBI's handling of the Nassar case, she revealed how being a victim of sexual abuse had increased the pressure she felt in Tokyo.

"If you looked at everything I've gone through for the past seven years, I should have never made another Olympic team," she told *New York Magazine*. "I should have quit way before Tokyo, when Larry Nassar was in the media for two years. It was too much."

"But I was not going to let him take something I've worked for since I was six years old. I wasn't going to let him take that joy away from me. So, I pushed past that for as long as my mind and my body would let me."

Nassar was sent to jail, but many abusers do not get charged, let alone convicted.

Child labour

The International Labour Organisation estimates that there are six million children working in forced labour.

And we are all guilty of encouraging because we are all consumers – and unwittingly consuming products that have their origins in slavery. Uncaringly might be a better word. Consumers are often unaware that slavery helps produce smartphones, laptops, shoes, chocolate, makeup, coffee and chic clothing brands.

Josephine Moulds wrote in the *Guardian*: "One of the biggest challenges in tackling child labour in the fashion supply chain is the complex supply chain for each garment. Even when brands have strict guidelines in place for suppliers, work often gets subcontracted to other factories that the buyer may not even know about." Sofie Ovaa, global campaign coordinator of Stop Child Labour, told Moulds that "companies that sell their products in Europe and the US have no clue where the textiles are sourced."

"A *Baptist World's Aids Behind the Barcode* report in 2015 found that 75% of 219 brands surveyed did not know the source of all their fabrics and inputs, and only half could trace where their products were cut and sewed," explained reporter Sass Brown.

A few countries do better than most religions. The Netherlands, for example, uses well-trained interviewers using a meticulous interview protocol with 14 separate questions related to a history of abuse. It shows that people's willingness to disclose a history of abuse is related to the interviewers' ability to demonstrate a sincere and sensitive interest.

Veterans and child soldiers – tough and yet vulnerable

To understand the trauma child soldiers face, it is worth looking at the legacy of Vietnam and the Falklands war.

American veterans make up just over 8% of the adult population but they account for 14% of all deaths by suicide. In the last decade, there has been an increase in the rate of suicide among younger Veterans.

When soldiers leave the military, they lose the structure and support they experienced during their service. This can lead to feelings of isolation, inadequacy, unrest, alienation, anxiety and lack of purpose. Close, intense relationships that are formed within units become disrupted and lost when deployment ends.

Mick Hermanis was one of 26,000 men and women who were sent from the United Kingdom to defend the Falkland Islands in 1982.

It took the British just three and a half weeks to defeat the Argentinians. They returned home to a heroes welcome.

But the trauma of fighting a war continues to affect them decades later. He said:

> "When you're 19, you're Superman – you can walk through walls, you are indestructible, you are the master of the universe, you've got everything in front of you."

BBC Panorama followed a group of former Welsh Guards, who have remained friends, as they flew 8,000 miles back to the Falklands to confront their demons for the first time in 35 years. As teenagers these men knew little of what they were getting themselves into. Yet their Falklands experience shaped their lives.

Hermanis survived the attack on the Sir Galahad landing ship – where the Welsh Guards suffered their heaviest losses, and where many of his friends died. This, combined with the fact that he never fired a bullet during the war, has left him with a strong feeling of survivor guilt.

On his return home from war, he said, "All the neighbours in the street were out and [I had] a bloody big hero's welcome."

He said it "broke my heart" to be given such a welcome when some of his mates would never return.

Mick was extremely nervous and apprehensive about returning to the Falklands. He had planned to go back in 2008 but bottled it at the last minute. "Not a single day that goes by when you don't think about it ... think about the boys ... friends that we lost ... some bloody fantastic boys."

Mick has had low moments, suffering from Post-Traumatic Stress Disorder (PTSD) and anger issues.

Nigel O'Keefe was 18 when he served in the infantry in the Falklands. At first, he says he "blanked" his experiences, "but as I grew older it started eating away at me." His defining memory was when his platoon found itself in one of the many minefields laid by the Argentinians. We were advancing, it was pitch black, there was tracer flying everywhere and a guy from the SAS came running out the single fire line and told everyone to stop – he said we're in a minefield.

"And as soon as he's told us that I could hear this screaming, high-pitched, really, really high-pitched screaming and I said, 'What the hell are women and kids doing out here?', like."

"I found out then it was two Royal Marines who'd stepped on anti-personnel mines."

"I've never heard a grown man scream so high-pitched like that."

Having never really addressed his PTSD and depression, he still suffers from terrible nightmares, and masks his problems with alcohol. It has caused him to lose both his job and his family; he is divorced and his four children rarely come to visit.

Nigel saw his trip back to the Falklands as his last chance to get his life back on track.

If professional soldiers suffer so much it is not surprising that when children become soldiers, it scars them deeply.

More than 250,000 children and adolescents are soldiers worldwide, almost half of them in Africa, according to the Office of the Special Representative of the Secretary-General for Children and Armed Conflict. These children are brutalized and cruelly abused by armed groups, and often forced to commit atrocities themselves. One key study comes from Northern Uganda. Since the late 1980s the area has been ravaged by the rebel terror of the Lord's Resistance Army (LRA). An estimated 25,000 children and adolescents have been recruited into the rebel forces (Coalition to Stop the Use of Child Soldiers, 2008). A quarter are girls.

Some of those interviewed had very normal ambitions. A 13-year-old boy said "I want to get married, buy a bicycle, and put up a building." A 15-year-old girl said, "I want to get a sewing machine so that I keep on making clothes and sell them to get some money. I will be a person who is responsible in the community; I will be an honest person; I will be a person who helps people."

Trauma survivors often experience survivor guilt and blame themselves (Kubany et al., 1996). They also suffer because they did things for which there was no justification. (Kubany, 1994). Survivors may also struggle with feelings of unfairness and injustice, and these can make them ruminate about revenge (Orth, Montada, and Maercker, 2006). Children said that the time spent with the armed group caused them pain and suffering and reported recurrent thoughts of their own acts being unjustified and unforgivable.

These responses can block cognitive change and so perpetuate PTSD. One problem is dissociations which trigger flashbacks to traumatic events, feeling disconnected from your own body, feeling disconnected from the world around you and in some dramatic cases, having multiple identities. The following have been shown to be risk factors for post-traumatic outcome in adults and children (Brewin 2009; Cook et al., 2003; Diseth, 2015; Ozer, Best, Lipsey, and Weiss, 2003).

Terr (1991) described four characteristics related to childhood trauma that do not fade with time; repeated intrusive memories of the traumatic event, repetitive behaviours, trauma-specific fears and altered attitudes towards people, life and the future.

Child soldiers are often forced to torture or kill other individuals, sometimes even their relatives, to survive. The will to survive, obedience to orders, seeing violence as normal and ideology may enable children to become perpetrators themselves (Wessells, 2005).

But the literature throws up a surprising finding. Klasen et al. (2010) interviewed 330 former Ugandan male and female child soldiers, aged 11–17. Though they had lived – and in some cases done – horrors, 27.6% were resilient. They did not have PTSD, depression and clinically significant behavioural and emotional problems. A number of factors helped. The resilient coped better because they were less exposed to domestic violence, were less plagued with guilt and were less inclined to seek revenge. Their families had a better socioeconomic situation and they felt they had more spiritual support. By contrast, children who were not resilient seemed to have what is being called developmental trauma disorder or DTD. Psychiatry has never been shy to posit a new condition. Key features of DTD are emotional dysregulation, disturbed attachment patterns, aggressive behaviour, and persistently altered attributions and expectancies. Sadly, valid self-report measurements are yet to be developed.

One trait seems to encourage resilience, finding a meaningful purpose in life, believing that one can influence one's surroundings and the outcome of events and trusting that one can learn and grow from both positive and negative life experiences (Kobasa et al., 1982). Hardiness is associated with post-traumatic adjustment (King et al., 1998). Also even if it sounds like a cliché, a positive orientation towards the future, being optimistic and having goals also help.

The late Sir Michael Rutter drew attention to the concept of resilience. An extensive literature shows parents and other supportive relationships foster resilience (Luthar, 2006; Masten et al., 2009). Children who have good caregivers fare better and young people who lose their parents are more vulnerable to psychopathology. Good relationships with parents and other adults appear to provide emotional security. As children grow older, relationships with friends and romantic partners increase in importance. One of the most devastating effects of adversity is the loss of the fundamental protections afforded by caring adults and friends, such as when parents are killed.

Klasen expected trauma severity when children were abducted would be a crucial predictor of post-traumatic outcome. However, this was not the case (Bayer et al., 2007). African extended family systems may have compensated for the loss of parents. The return of children from the often extremely traumatizing experiences with the rebels to a violent and rejecting home environment may have led to an ultimate loss of trust in other people. There is some evidence that the exposure to war violence might brutalize societies and facilitate domestic abuse (Catani et al., 2008). Therefore, violent behaviour within families and communities might emerge as a long-term effect of warfare lasting beyond the end of armed conflict. Far more research needs to be done.

The clergy often abuse boys and girls but in war faith helps. Children who did not feel abandoned by God during crises showed significantly fewer symptoms. Spirituality and Christian religion are deeply rooted in Northern Ugandans and may therefore be an important source of healing and reconciliation (Harlacher et al., 2006). Again this needs to be further investigated.

Klasen's finding that revenge motivation was a risk factor for worse post-traumatic outcome is consistent with other research (Bayer et al., 2007). Those who want revenge are not inclined to reconciliation and forgiveness, also in child soldiers (Bayer et al., 2007; McCullough et al., 2001). Overcoming revenge motives may therefore be a crucial step.

In South Africa two years after Nelson Mandela became president there was a serious attempt at reconciliation to help remedy the injustices of apartheid. The Truth and Reconciliation Commission hoped to deal with the thousands of human rights violations that had taken place including the Sharpeville massacre. At the Nuremberg trials leading Nazis were either sentenced to death or jailed. Reconciliation was not possible with them. The South African Commission had to work in a country which was not occupied by conquerors. The whites had lost absolute power, but the country still had to work. In one study, the effectiveness of the Commission was measured on a variety of levels:

- Its usefulness in terms of confirming what had happened during the apartheid regime ("bringing out the truth")
- The feelings of reconciliation that could be linked to the Commission
- The positive effects (both domestically and internationally) that the Commission brought about (i.e. in the political and the economic environment of South Africa)

Lentini examined the opinions of three ethnic groups: the British Africans, the Afrikaners and the Xhosa. All of them thought the Commission was effective in bringing out the truth, but to varying degrees, depending on the group in question.

Some viewed the evidence given as not entirely accurate, as many people would lie in order to keep themselves out of trouble while receiving amnesty for their crimes. Some said that the proceedings only helped to remind them of the horrors that had taken place in the past when they had been working to forget such things. The real question is what can be learned in trying to reconcile other conflicts.

Klasen calls for longitudinal research. Better understanding would help psychological rehabilitation for war-affected children.

Gender differences

The association of being a child soldier status with PTSD was twice as strong for girls compared with boys. This suggests that factors such as non-traumatic child soldier experiences or traumatic exposures other than those the teams assessed may contribute to depression and PTSD, with these factors especially important for girl soldiers.

One aspect of this research is curious: the study assumes that boys reported significantly more traumatic events during conscription than girls, as girls were more frequently assigned domestic chores, e.g. cooking and caring for younger children, while boys were primarily sent to fight, loot and abduct civilians. There turned out to be few gender differences, however, that might be explained, Klassen said by the fact that girl might have assigned domestic chores, though that did not protect them from repeated sexual assaults, group assaults and getting pregnant.

Klasen's work in Uganda echoes some of the results of Betancourt in Sierra Leone. She interviewed four times – in 2002, 2004, 2008 and 2016 to 2017 – about their involvement with armed groups, exposure to violence in the war and about their family and community relationships after the war.

Nearly half the respondents reported anxiety and depression, with 28% suffering from post-traumatic stress disorder, according to her recent report, titled "Stigma and Acceptance of Sierra Leone's Child Soldiers: A Prospective Longitudinal Study of Adult Mental Health and Social Functioning." Betancourt identified three groups:

- The Socially Protected group, nearly two-thirds of the respondents, reported they were not heavily stigmatized for their involvement in conflict. Their families and communities largely accepted them. This group reported largely that they had lower levels of exposure to wartime violence.
- The Improving Social Integration group included respondents who in 2002 reported high levels of stigmatization and low rates of acceptance. This group, largely female and more likely to have been raped, have since reported a decrease in stigma and increase in acceptance by families and communities.
- The Socially Vulnerable group – roughly 10% of the respondents – reported adverse mental health outcomes and only

slight improvements from 2002. This group is largely male, and crucially spent more time in fighting forces and were more likely to have killed or injured others during the war.

Members of the socially vulnerable group were about twice as likely as those in the socially protected group to experience high levels of anxiety and depression. They were three times more likely to have attempted suicide and over four times more likely to have been in trouble with the police.

"There is healing power in the relationships young people build within their families and communities," said Betancourt, who directs the Research Program on Children and Adversity at BC. "What these latest findings show is that just as much attention should be paid to family and community relationships as to the traumatic events of their past. Efforts to alleviate mental health problems and improve life outcomes for former child soldier need to focus much more on family and community relationships."

"Conducting a study like this over so many years in Sierra Leone is a real challenge," said co-author and Research Program on Children and Adversity statistician, Robert T. Brennan. "Addresses are approximate, birthdays, even ages, are often unknown, and natural disasters displace whole communities. We even had to postpone data collection due to the Ebola outbreak of 2014 to 2015."

"Because this study follows a single cohort of former child soldiers – some as young as 10 years old – into young adulthood, it is certain to be a landmark in the study of the exploitation of children by armed groups," said Boston College School of Social Work Dean, Gautam N. Yadama.

The Taliban

African wars get less coverage than Afghanistan where the Taliban have been recruiting children as soldiers for 20 years.

Jihad, the war they have been waging, is a holy war and the Taliban view seems to be that boys deserve the chance to wage it.

The Taliban's apparent strategy to throw increasing numbers of children into battle is cynical, cruel and also unlawful.

Human Rights Watch interviewed relatives of 13 children recruited as Taliban soldiers. Despite Taliban claims that they only enlist fighters who have achieved "mental and physical maturity," and do not use "boys with no beards" in military operations, some of the children recruited from madrasas in Kunduz, Takhar and Badakhshan provinces are 13 or younger. Despite the evidence the Taliban have previously denied "the use of children and adolescents in Jihadic Operations."

Kunduz residents say that the increase in recruitment and deployment of child fighters coincided with the Taliban's major offensive in northern Afghanistan that began in April 2015. Human Rights Watch interviews with activists and analysts make clear that the Taliban-run madrasas have been functioning in Kunduz, as well as other northern provinces, since at least 2012.

Taliban commanders use madrasas not only for indoctrination, but also for military training. Boys begin indoctrination as young as six years old and continue to study religious subjects under Taliban teachers for up to seven years. According to relatives of boys recruited by the Taliban, by the time they are 13, Taliban-educated children have learned how to drill, shoot and the production and deployment of IEDs. Taliban teachers then introduce those trained child soldiers to specific Taliban groups in that district.

More than 100 children recruited from one district alone in Kunduz told Human Watch that it was easy to convince them of the righteousness of jihad. If famliles tried to rescue boys they were told the boys had joined of their own free will. Money also plays a part as the Taliban pay expenses and provide food.

Some of the cases histories are revealing –

- Ahmad was the son of a merchant in Chahardara district. In May 2015, when he was 14 years old, Taliban forces under a senior Taliban commander, Commander B, recruited Ahmad as a soldier. About a week after her son was recruited, Ahmad's mother appealed to Commander B to release her son, but he refused

Mohammad joined the Taliban over his father's objections. He is currently a fighter in Commander B's group. His parents together with local elders went to the Taliban several times and asked another commander in this group, Commander C, to free Mohammad. Commander C then asked Farhad if he wanted to go back to his family, but as Qari Farhad wanted to stay, Commander C told his parents and other local elders that "your sons are better Muslims than yourselves." The elders did not believe in jihad.

Qari Burhan – After he was recruited, he was sent to Waziristan (in Pakistan) to be trained in using explosive materials. He came back to the front after three months of training in July 2015 and is active in Commander B's armed group.

- Navid, 16, is a resident of Kunduz centre. According to his family, he has been made part of commander B's bodyguard. He sits at the back of a Taliban commander.

Freud posited the death wish after the end of the First World War. There is much evidence of it now and the victims are often young.

Suicide bombers – and those who order children to kill themselves

Ariel Merari of Tel Aviv University had access to 15 would-be suicide bombers being held in jail for attempted attacks relating to the Israeli-Palestinian conflict. He and his team also interviewed the organisers of suicide attacks and a control group – 12 men who had been tried and jailed for various political violence activities from stone-throwing to armed assaults.

The first challenge was to get them speak. Merari said:

> "I told them why we wanted to carry out this project, this study," explained Professor Merari on Radio 4's All in the Mind.

"There was real lively discussion. In the end they agreed to participate and that was indeed the key to achieving the consent of the other organisers."

Merari wanted to see if suicide bombers shared any noticeable personality traits or characteristics. He talked to the men and often boys who had tried to carry out a suicide attack but had failed for a variety of reasons, including technical defects (the bomb did not go off) or capture (either on the way to the target or earlier). The Tel Aviv team discovered a pattern of being unable to handle stressful situations, an inability to see the bigger picture and a tendency to be intimidated by people in positions of authority. Put simply they were often inadequate.

Meanwhile, the organisers – responsible for commanding others to kill and in the process die had bigger egos – were better equipped mentally to handle stress and, for the most part, were unwilling to consider a suicide attack themselves.

Suicide attacks are often tied to a perception of religious fanaticism from the perpetrator.

"Almost all of them were religious, but the suicide guys were not more religious than the control group members."

"The depth or intensity of religious belief was not something which distinguished them from other non-suicide terrorists."

Merari found that "national humiliation" ranked higher as a reason for an attack.

"This was by far the clearest, strongest motivation they expressed. It is not a matter of personal suffering; they tried to avenge their communities suffering. They mentioned events that they saw on television, not events that happened to them personally."

The organisers were, on average, older, better educated and, perhaps predictably, unlikely to put themselves forward for suicide attacks.

"Nine of 14 admitted that they would not be willing to carry out suicide attacks themselves – because they were afraid," said Merari. "They did not use the term 'afraid', but they use terms such as 'not everybody can carry out an act such as this', 'it takes a special person'. He did not study suggestibility."

"The remaining five said 'In principle I would be willing to carry it out, but my role as a commander was more important and therefore I did not do it'. They were frank, I guess, in giving this straightforward answer."

The organisers' portrayal of suicide bombers as being "highly determined youngsters" was misguided.

"The suicide [bombers] themselves gave a very different picture. Sixty-six per cent of them admitted that they were afraid, they hesitated, and when we looked at larger number of suicide cases we found that 36% of 61 cases of suicide bombers the candidates just dropped out."

Merari acknowledges that because his subjects all "failed" their mission, the study cannot offer an exact representation of a suicide bomber. Nevertheless, his team believes that their findings are as "close as possible" to the truth. "Some of our suicide bombers actually got to their target and pressed the switch – just that the bomb they were carrying failed to explode because of mechanical failure."

"Psychologically, these are suicide bombers for all effects and purposes."

He concluded that measures can be taken to prevent attacks based on the common personality traits.

"One of the conclusions of this study was that any impediment on the way to the target increases the chance that the suicide bomber would change his mind. This is because those who hesitate need some sort of excuse."

"They have to have some sort of excuse to keep their self-respect."

"Any kind of impediment, statistically, would increase the chance that the would-be suicide bomber changes his mind on the way to the target."

Perhaps the last word should go to Anand Gopal, the author of *No Good Men Among the Living: America, the Taliban and the War Through Afghan Eyes* which describes the travails of three Afghans caught in the war on terror. It was a finalist for the 2015 Pulitzer Prize for general non-fiction.

Anand found that many of the young Taliban members who recently surged into Kabul and cities and towns all over Afghanistan were not even born when 9/11 happened and most of them did not even know about 9/11. "You know, they'll say, Yeah, there was some attack in the U.S.A., but they don't really link 9/11 to what's happened in their country for the last twenty years," he told *The New Yorker*.

When they were asked why the Americans were in Afghanistan, they gave all sorts of reasons, from, you know, "Oh, we have minerals here and, you know, the Soviets wanted our precious metals, and now the U.S. does, too." They added, "They just hate our way of life," which always struck him as interesting because that was the frame that we're using on 9/11 here in the United States. And, of course, it's different when you get to the edge – you know, the sort of more élite Taliban, who follow the news – but I'm, I'm talking about the rank-and-file Taliban. They really don't see their conflict, or their struggle, as having anything to do with September 11th.

Having explored the celebrities and the suffering, it is time to turn to fairy tales which often emphasise children seek justice – for themselves and others.

Chapter 10

Fairy Tales and Children's TV: Weak Children Who Become Strong

The biologist Edward O Wilson and the psychologist Michael Tomasello independently stress the fact that the development of language made collaboration possible. It also allowed parents to show love for their children. Most parents like reading to their children when they are tucking them into bed and there is much evidence that this is a good experience for both. The children's book market is vast as a result and has produced such bestsellers as the "Mr Men series," "the Gruffalo" and for older children, the "Harry Potter series." Harry Potter's appeal stems from the fact that he is a persecuted boy as a result of losing both his parents.

Many folk and fairy tales – academics do differentiate between the two – are tales of children winning through. Their heroines and heroes are often children who develop the strength to overcome obstacles.

In 1697, Charles Perrault published one of the first collections of folk and fairy tales. He excluded some of the gorier examples to make them acceptable to the French court which he served. A century later the Grimm brothers began to collect folk tales; they assumed that fairy tales and myths represented a purer, more authentic mode of German thinking. Fairy tales whisk the hero or heroine into an enchanted space. They often need to escape a problem – what to do with an unwanted child; how to find a wife; who will succeed to the throne – but a tale may also be a scarier adventure where the hero seeks forbidden knowledge. Some tales are dark and deal with incest, abandonment and even murder. Through the tales the hero or heroine often grows – and grows up.

Some children's stories can be nihilistic too. "Ten Little Sausages" is a tale of sausage after sausage jumping into a frying

DOI: 10.4324/9781003165484-11

pan till "there were none." That is also the title of an Agatha Christie book in which ten people are killed on a windswept island; all of them, unlike the sausages, had gotten away with murder.

Psychoanalysts have approached fairy tales from three perspectives. Freud and Jung considered they were relics of primitive thought that could be mined to reveal original traumas.

The second perspective is clinical. Analysts quickly applied the Freudian method of dream analysis to fairy tales. Like dreams, these stories seemed to capture usually inaccessible symbols, bringing them closer to consciousness.

Freud wrote a brief paper in *The Occurrence in Dreams of Material from Fairy Tales* in 1913. He confirmed the importance of fairy tales to the developing mental life of children, to the point that recollections of an adult's favourite fairy tales can distort or usurp their own childhood recollections: "they have made the fairy tales into screen memories," he wrote. A screen memory is a distorted usually visual memory. Fairy tales were tools the analyst could use to decipher the secrets of the unconscious. In them complex struggles are played out by a simple cast, figures of instinct rather than characters with history and memory. Fairy tales are raw manifestations of desire and fear.

Carl Jung (1960) claimed we all had both a personal unconscious, and a collective unconscious whose contents were symbolic. He called these archetypes. These tend "to form such representations of a motif – representations that can vary a great deal in detail without losing their basic pattern" (Jung, 1964, p. 67). We do not know and are never conscious of them, but they can generate images and symbols.

For Jung, fairy tales connect with the Collective Unconscious and therefore are psychic evidence of the very first order. The heroes or heroines of fairy tales are abstractions – that is archetypes. Fairy tales are the purest and simplest expression of collective unconscious psychic processes. Therefore, their value for the scientific investigation of the unconscious exceeds that of all other materials. They represent the archetypes in their simplest, barest and most concise form and give the best clues to the understanding of the processes going on in the collective psyche.

Transformation is often the climax and point of a tale. In one story by the brothers, Grimm Dummling jumps into the pond which enables her to transform into a beautiful woman, what this means is "Acceptance of the frog and the frog's life implies a jump into the inner world, sinking down into an inner reality ..." (p. 98). There's a wonderfully daft Russian version cited here in which the frog princess conceals food up her sleeves and as she dances: "she waves her right arm and out of it falls a bit of the food, which is transformed into a garden with a pillar in it. Around this a tomcat circles, then climbs up it and sings folk songs. When it comes down it tells fairy tales. In this way you see even more clearly that the anima creates the symbolic life, for she transforms ordinary food for the body into spiritual food through creating art and mythological tales; she restores paradise, a kind of archetypal world of fantasy. The tomcat represents a nature spirit which is the creator of folk songs and fairy tales. It also shows the close connection of the anima with man's capacity for artistic work and with the fantasy world."

Freud disagreed with Jung on many issues but not on this. Freud wrote: "Dream-symbolism extends far beyond dreams: it is not peculiar to dreams but exercises a similar dominating influence on representation in fairy-tales, myths and legends, in jokes and in folk-lore" (Freud 1901, p. 685). In Freud's paper on fairy tales (1913a), he interpreted fairy tale material found in dreams as personal associations in two individual patients. In his analysis of the Wolf Man, he details his patient's dream of six or seven white wolves sitting in a tree and the dreamer's great fear of being eaten. When Freud asks for associations to the dream, the Wolf Man thinks of a picture from Little Red Riding Hood of a large bold wolf. The tree then reminds him of another folk story, about a tailor who pulls off the tail of a wolf when he is attacked. The tailless wolf is evidence of the castration complex, Freud writes. The Wolf Man then associates again to another fairy tale, "The Wolf and the Seven Little Goats" where six little goats are eaten by the wolf after their mother had gone away, and only the seventh escapes.

Early psychoanalysts were also interested in interpretation as a tool for the study of literature. Freud was an avid reader and used as sources folk epics; Grimms' Fairy Tales; Greek, Roman, Germanic myths and Shakespeare's *The Merchant of Venice*. There Bassanio, in his speech defending his choice of the lead casket, speaks of the metal's paleness, to which Freud adds "lead is dumb" (p. 294). For him dumbness is equated with death. In the Grimms' tale, *The Twelve Brothers*, the heroine, to save her brothers from death, must remain "dumb" for seven years.

There are also analyses of "The Three Feathers" from both von Franz, a Jungian, and Bettelheim, a Freudian. Both say that the fairy tale provides meaning. Bettelheim argued that fairy tales help children solve existential problems such as separation anxiety, oedipal conflict and sibling rivalries. The extreme violence and ugly emotions of many fairy tales are fantasies that help the child deal with anxieties in her or his life. A child's unrealistic fears often require unrealistic hopes. The key for von Franz is making contact with the primal unconscious: "Psychological interpretation is our way of telling stories; we still have the same need and we still crave the renewal that comes from understanding archetypal images" (p. 32).

In *the Uses of Enchantment* Bettelheim saw fairy tales as the setting for Oedipal battles – and sometimes for sibling rivalry. He said that he was writing the book as "an educator and therapist of severely disturbed children."

It is worth looking at his analysis of some tales in particular.

Cinderfuckin'rella

In *Pretty Woman* when the heroine asks her friend if there is any precedent for a girl suddenly finding herself in five star luxury in a top Hollywood hotel, her friend perks up Cinderfuckin'rella. The story of Cinderella first appeared in China in the 9th century where foot binding was considered erotic. The link with the slipper, Bettelheim claimed, was clear. Cinderella did not find happiness easily. In some versions she had to wriggle out of her father's desire to marry her. Vice is nice but incest is best is an old two-liner which suggests forces work against the incest taboo. Then Cinderella was made to live among ashes which unsurprisingly is a mark of degradation. No other fairy tale, Bettelheim argued, evokes so well the sense of a child at the mercy of older brothers and sisters, not to mention appalling parents and the inevitable cruel stepmother.

Bettelheim traces the child's misery to the fact that "before oedipal entanglements" the child is sure he is loved and lovable and the "oedipal disappointments," which then make the child feel that there must be some serious flaw in her or him. She needs assurance at a conscious and unconscious level that she "will able to extricate himself from these predicaments." One of the greatest merits of Cinderella is that the fairy godmother is critical for in the tale "the child understands that it essentially through her own efforts and because she is the person she that she can transcend magnificently her degraded state." Cinderella conquers her oedipal disappointments, defeats her ugly sisters, marries the prince and lives happily ever after. At the end of *Pretty Woman,* when Richard Gere asks Julia Roberts what happens after the prince rescues the princess, she puts back that she rescues him right back.

Goldilocks

The story of the three bears was well known before the publication of the poet Robert Southey's tale. In 1813, he was telling the story to friends. In his version three bears – "a little, small, wee bear, a middle-sized bear, and a great, huge bear" – live together in a house in the woods. Each of these "bachelor" bears has his own porridge bowl, chair and bed. One day the porridge is too hot to eat, so they decide to take a walk in the woods while their porridge cools. An old woman comes to the bears' house. She has been exiled by her family because she is a disgrace to them. She is impudent, bad, foul-mouthed, ugly, dirty, a no good nik. She looks through a window, peeps through the keyhole and lifts the latch. She eats the Wee Bear's porridge, then settles into his chair and breaks it. Prowling about, she finds the bears' beds and falls asleep in Wee Bear's bed. When the bears return. Wee Bear cries, "Somebody has been lying in my bed, and here she is!" The old woman wakes, jumps out the window and is never seen again.

The story hit a nerve as many retellings show. In 1831 Eleanor Mure made the intruder not a pretty blonde but an old woman. Southey and Mure differ in many details. Southey's bears have porridge, while Mure's have milk; Southey's old woman has no motive for entering the house, but Mure's old woman is piqued when her courtesy visit is rebuffed; Southey's old woman runs away when discovered, but Mure's old woman is impaled on the steeple of St Paul's *Cathedral.* A splendid end.

Goldilocks' fate varies in the many retellings: in some versions, she runs into the forest, in some others she is almost eaten by the bears but her mother rescues her, in some she vows to be a good child, and in some she returns home.

Goldilocks and the Three Bears both offer good examples of how fairy tales tell children they can acquire power. Twelve years after Southey published the tale, Joseph Cundall turned the ugly old woman to a pretty little girl in his *Treasury of Pleasure Books for*

Young Children. He explained his reasons for doing so in a dedicatory letter to his children, dated November 1849, which was inserted at the beginning of the book:

The "Story of the Three Bears" is a very old Nursery Tale, but it was never so well told as by the great poet Southey, whose version I have (with permission) given you, only I have made the intruder a little girl instead of an old woman. This I did because I found that the tale is better known with *Silver Hair*, and because there are so many other stories of old women.

Cundall set a trend. Goldilocks also got many new names like Silver Hair in the pantomime *Harlequin and The Three Bears; or, Little Silver Hair* or Silver-Locks in *Aunt Mavor's Nursery Tales* (1858) or Golden Hair in *Aunt Friendly's Nursery Book* (ca. 1868).

Today the blonde often features in shampoo ads. Then the wonderful film *Gentlemen Prefer Blondes* is all about men falling for blondes. It stars Marilyn Monroe who, of course, all the men lust after.

Bettelheim described Goldilocks as "poor, beautiful, and charming," and notes that the story does not describe her positively except for her hair. In his view, the tale fails to encourage children "to pursue the hard work of solving the problems which growing up presents." Goldilocks is a porridge thief and bed intruder. The story does not end as fairy tales should with the "promise of future happiness awaiting those who have mastered their Oedipal situation as a child." Bettelheim believes the tale is an escapist one that thwarts the child reading it from gaining emotional maturity.

The key for Bettelheim is consolation. For him fairy tales speak to existential fears in all of us – desertion, loneliness, sexual attraction, becoming an adult: "Today, even more than in past times, the child needs the reassurance offered by the image of the isolated man who nevertheless." Bettelheim understands a generational conflict. The boy hero feels small and inferior to his father; he struggles with both admiration and rivalry, wanting to be big and possess a woman like his father.

Bettelheim sees the fairy tale as a kind of road map of navigating from adolescence into adulthood.

In the United States, Bettelheim and *The Uses of Enchantment* won the 1976 *National Book Critics Circle Award* for Criticism among other awards. Robert A. Segal praised, "It is the disjunction between Bettelheim's up-to-date approach to fairy tales and his old-fashioned approach to myths that is striking."

But unlike most fairy tales, there was no happy ending. In the Winter 1991 edition of the *Journal of American Folklore*, Alan Dundes, then a 28-year veteran in the anthropology department at the University of California, Berkeley, accused Bettelheim of copying key passages from *A Psychiatric Study of Myths and Fairy Tales: Their Origin, Meaning, and Usefulness* (1963, 1974 rev. ed.) by Julius Heuscher without giving appropriate credit, as well as unacknowledged borrowing from other

Peter Pan and other tales

A quick flip through some ever-popular fairy tales reveals many instances where children become strong and clever. As we shall see I cannot resist putting a modern spin into the descriptions. Peter Pan is a free-spirited and mischievous boy who enters the Darling family's nursery. The children are soon whisked away on an adventure where they have to confront the dreaded Captain Hook, his gang of pirates and the crocodile at whom we must never smile. Are the children beaten by them? Naturally not. It is the pirates who walk the plank while the crocodile in some modern versions is turned into a luxury handbag.

At least Cinderella was not in danger of being eaten as the three little pigs were. The big, bad wolf imagines wolfing them down for breakfast. The first little piggy and the second little piggy don't fare well, but the third little piggy builds his house out of brick, so it is strong enough to withstand the hungry wolf's huffs and puffs.

Hansel and Gretel are left in the woods to find their way to a house made of sweets, Gretel has to rescue her brother Hansel from the wicked witch.

When Little Red Riding Hood realises that the creature in her grandmother's bed is not her grandma, but a greedy wolf eager to eat her up, she quickly devises a plan to outwit him.

Iona and Peter Opie point out in *The Classic Fairy Tales* (1999) that the tale has a "partial analogue" in "*Snow White*": the lost princess enters the dwarfs' house, tastes their food and falls asleep in one of their beds. Like the three bears, the dwarfs cry, "Someone's been sitting in my chair!", "Someone's been eating off my plate!" and "Someone's been sleeping in my bed!" The Opies also point to similarities in a Norwegian tale about a princess who takes refuge in a cave inhabited by three Russian princes dressed in bearskins. She eats their food and hides under a bed.

When the Grimm brothers wrote no one worried about climate change. Among much else it will take imagination to get to net zero. In that spirit a fairy tale for Climate Change might be nice.

The Green Queen

The heroine is the Green Queen but she is not binary as she is up to date. She can change into the Green King and, when she has had enough of being sort of human, into the last dinosaur who somehow survived when a giant asteroid rammed the earth. She lives in a forest and knows that if she is to save the people there, she has to persuade them to abandon many habits. They have to break up their motor cars and relearn Tarzan's old habit of swinging from branch to branch. They have to stop chopping down trees. Their personal habits also have to change. Less meat on the men please. They also have to forego deodorants, a product invented by the founder of behaviourism John B Watson who had to leave academia when he had an affair with one of his students. He went into advertising and persuaded people they had to cover normal smells. The Green Queen also wants people to have fewer hot baths. As they return to a state of nature, they need to change their wardrobe too. They must learn to be happy if they have two shirts, two trousers and two underpants and two bras. All this fashion stuff damages the earth. Not using washing machines and dryers will also help. Needless to say the forest dwellers say all this would make them uncivilised. Maybe though these are sacrifices we will have to make to survive.

That reminds us of Mahatma Gandhi who did not have a selection of loincloths. When he was asked what he thought of Western civilisation he said it would be a good idea. Unfortunately no one has been able to confirm the quote.

Western civilisation, of course, is what children are taught in Western schools.

Chapter 11

The Challenge to Education

In my schooldays which now seem pre-historic, you listened to the teacher and took notes which you were expected to regurgitate on demand. Only if you were intelligent did you dare comment. And woe betides you if you put a foot wrong. In the 1960s the comedy *Whacko* featured Jimmy Edwards as a teacher who relished every opportunity to cane his pupils. At my prep school we suffered a master who took every opportunity to whack us with a Jokari bat while the maths master, who still called himself Colonel 18 years after the war ended, used to flick matches at our heads hoping to set our hair on fire. When I did history A level, there was no discussion of contemporary politics.

Perhaps the most crucial difference was that pupils had no power then. The teacher's rule was law. There was no question of feedback, no Rate Your Teacher questions, whereas now pupils are expected to leave comments which the teachers have to read. In the past pupils just had to put up with whatever teaching they got.

Did caning win wars?

English schools were caning, even flogging, children for centuries and it has been argued that this was why we won wars. The French and Germans did not really know how to cane their young.

George Orwell described how he was punished after wetting his bed at his prep school Saint Cyprian's. After the latest incident, he wrote in *Oh Those were the Joys* he was told:

> "REPORT YOURSELF to the Headmaster after breakfast!"

DOI: 10.4324/9781003165484-12

Orwell put REPORT YOURSELF in capitals because that was how it appeared in his mind. "The words always had a portentous sound in my ears, like muffled drums or the words of the death sentence."

The headmaster Sambo took a bone-handled riding-crop out of the cupboard, "but it was part of the punishment of reporting yourself that you had to proclaim your offence with your own lips. When I had said my say, he read me a short but pompous lecture, then seized me by the scruff of the neck, twisted me over and began beating me with the riding crop. He had a habit of continuing his lecture while he flogged you, and I remember the words "you dir-ty lit-tle boy" keeping time with the blows. The beating did not hurt (perhaps, as it was the first time, he was not hitting me very hard), and I walked out feeling very much better. The fact that the beating had not hurt was a sort of victory and partially wiped out the shame of the bed-wetting. I was even incautious enough to wear a grin on my face. Some small boys were hanging about in the passage outside the door of the ante-room.

> "D'you get the cane?"
> "It didn't hurt. I said proudly."
> Flip, the matron, had heard everything and screamed.
> "Come here! Come here this instant! What was that you said?"
> "I said it didn't hurt," I faltered out.
> "How dare you say a thing like that? Do you think that is a proper thing to say? Go in and REPORT YOURSELF AGAIN!"

This time Sambo laid on in real earnest. He continued for a length of time that frightened and astonished me – about five minutes, it seemed – ending up by breaking the riding crop. The bone handle went flying across the room.

"Look what you've made me do!" he said furiously, holding the broken crop.

Today Sambo would be dismissed and probably arrested. In higher education today many lecturers complain that students are now called clients or consumers, and clients have the right to rate their teachers. Many lecturers feel they have to kow tow to a new normal where the young have more power than ever before and use it sometimes unwisely. The situation leads to conflict. School students have led the way on climate protests as they challenge the complacency of established politicians. Their protests have led sometimes to threats and punishment. The punishments range from being given after-school detention for taking part in local strikes, were marked as truant or even suspended. The lecturers feel under pressure often to give high marks for work that does not deserve it. Some of my family and friends are lecturers and are annoyed by this to say the least.

If – the school revolt

Fiction got there first. Lindsay Anderson's If was a brilliant film made in 1968 set in a public school. Mick and Johnny sneak off the school grounds and steal a motorbike from a showroom. Later, the three boys drink vodka in their study and consider how one man holds the potential to "change the world with a bullet in the right place." Their clashes with school authorities become increasingly contentious. Eventually, a brutal caning spurs them to action.

During a school Combined Cadet Force military drill, Mick steals live ammunition, which he and two other boys use to open fire on a group of boys and masters.

As punishment, the trio is ordered by the headmaster to clean out a large storeroom beneath the main school hall. In a surreal sequence, they discover a cache of firearms.

On Founders' Day, when parents are visiting the school, the group starts a fire under the hall, smoking everyone out of the building. They then open fire on them from the rooftop. Led by a visiting General who was giving a speech, the staff, students and parents break open the Combined Cadet Force armoury and begin firing back. The headmaster tries to stop the fight, imploring the group to listen to reason. In response, he is shot between the eyes. The battle continues, and the camera closes in on Mick's determined face as he keeps firing.

The TikTok battle

Recent videos on TikTok encourage children to vandalise school bathrooms and even attack teachers on camera.

Along with "slap a teacher" trend, videos tagged "deck the halls and show your b***s" for December has also been making its way around the social media site. Some children have been found setting up fake school TikTok accounts and posting inappropriate videos.

Now councillors in North Wales are asking parents to check their children's mobile phones and social media accounts to make sure any inappropriate videos have been deleted. Some schools are also taking it upon themselves to monitor pupils' social media and warn they "will take the necessary action" if content filmed on school grounds is found.

Cllr Huw Hilditch-Roberts, who is the cabinet member for education in Denbighshire, spoke out against the worrying new trends. He said:

> "These national trends – like the ice bucket challenge – do gain momentum. We want to make sure and ask parents to check that, if children are on TikTok, they are the legal age to be on it."
>
> "We understand that children engage with social media, but we don't want anybody else to suffer on the back of it."

The councillor then declared war on pupils, especially those who wanted to wreck bathrooms and "smack a staff member." The Council was calling in the police and writing to parents warning that: "It has come to our attention that some learners in our secondary schools have been making short films and uploading them on the TikTok app whilst in schools." This was forbidden as was filming on school premises without permission.

"The local authority has asked schools to remind pupils that learners are not allowed to upload unauthorised short films in the name of their school."

"In all cases, we have asked schools to consider appropriate sanctions for those learners who have filmed and uploaded inappropriate material involving school staff and pupils whilst on school premises."

So the classroom risks becoming a war zone.

History versus politics

Philips (2002) examined the ways in which the history curriculum in UK schools has been contested and considers the implications of the impact of postmodernism – particularly consumption – upon history teaching. He explored the relationship between "official history" taught in schools and the "unofficial histories" which influence children.

Yuen (2007) argued the Beijing government has repeatedly emphasised the development of national identity and patriotism. One of the locations where these issues might be expected to appear is in the teaching of Government and Public Affairs (GPA), an optional subject offered to secondary students aged 15–18. The findings show that the teachers understand national identity and patriotism critically. They insist politics should be taught in a rational way. At the same time, they think teaching politics in a rational way, with no appeal to the emotions as is the current practice, will enhance neither the students' sense of national identity nor their patriotism.

In the United Kingdom, young people get their political literacy from their life experiences (like Marcus Rashford, who lived through child hunger) or in higher education. There is no mandatory political education in the United Kingdom. This means that all young people who impact democracy, are doing so as anomalies or outliers.

A survey by Shout Out United Kingdom found that more than 70% of students would welcome the creation of a Government and Politics GCSE, the group aims to focus discussions between young people, teachers, civil society organisations and parliamentarians from both Houses around the idea.

In February 2021, the Director of Shout Out, Matteo Bergamini said, "Young people have the power to make immense and positive change in the world – I have always believed that. Given the right direction and with the right information in hand, young people have the potential to shape a better world – Greta Thunberg, Jack Andraka, Emma González and Malala Yousafzai are just a handful of names that spring to mind."

Simon Fell MP, Co-Chair and Registered Contact, said, "There has never been a better time to be talking to young people about political engagement. We live in an era of fake news and we need to fight back against that by giving young people the tools to be better and more informed. I'm delighted to be co-chairing the group from its launch and look forward to engaging with young people to hear their views on this important subject."

In the USA only nine states and the District of Columbia require one year of US government or civics, while 30 states require a half year and the other 11 states have no civics requirement. While federal education policy has focused on improving academic achievement in reading and math, this has come at the expense of a broader curriculum. Most states have dedicated insufficient class time to understanding the basic functions of government.

State civics curricula are heavy on knowledge but light on building skills and agency for civic engagement. An examination of standards for civics and US government courses found that 32 states and the District of Columbia provide instruction on American democracy and other systems of government, the history of the Constitution and Bill of Rights, an explanation of mechanisms for public participation, and instruction on state and local voting policies. However, no state has experiential learning or local problem-solving components in its civics requirements.

Chapter 12

Sex – Children Are More Knowing, but More Exploited, Than Ever

In his *The History of My Life*, Casanova described how he lost his virginity at the age of 11. This was not unusual in Venice in the 1730s. Strangely Freud was less aware of the eddies of history when he observed 125 years ago that children were sexual beings. Boys who touched their willies were often told that if they did that again it would be cut off even though it is normal.

Carl Rogers is remembered as the originator of humanistic psychotherapy, but he started his career in the 1920s working with delinquent children. At the time children were meant to know nothing about sex. Heading a charity in upstate New York, he was surprised to find that some 10- and 11-year-old boys knew far more about the forbidden subject than decency expected. His colleagues did not appreciate his discoveries – psychologists often feared their science would be seen as too interested in sex so he stopped working with children, moved to a new university and decided to work with adults.

Children today reflect increasing sexualisation. The American Association of Paediatrics lists some behaviours as normal for under five-year-olds. These are showing their genitals to others, trying to look at naked people and masturbating. However it claims the following behaviours are highly abnormal at six years old or above. They include putting mouth on genitals, asking self/others to engage in specific sex acts, imitating intercourse, inserting objects into the vagina or anus, touching animal genitals.

Also children are often exposed to nudity in the media and to pornography. The American Academy of Paediatrics notes, "American media is thought to be the most sexually suggestive in

DOI: 10.4324/9781003165484-13

the Western Hemisphere. The average American adolescent will view nearly 14,000 sexual references per year."

TV and the internet shower information and titillation. Curiously magazines such as Teen Breathe and Kookie offer mindfulness for the young whereas 20 years ago magazines were full of dating advice. Still, sex education is often just biological. Only half of 18–25s who had received sex education reported that they had been given information on sexual feelings, relationships and emotions. Thirty-five per cent of young people were given information on homosexuality, 66% on safer sex and STIs and 70% on contraception. Parents' and teachers' discomfort in talking about these topics may mean young people lack knowledge about them. Both teenagers and parents can find it hard to communicate openly and effectively about sex and relationships.

Health care professionals look more than before for signs children have been exposed to sexual behaviour. Past child-on-child sexual behaviours, which may have been minimized by society, are now taken seriously.

Psychologists have found that children between the ages of 12 and 14 abuse other children. This is the time when children experience many changes as puberty begins, and if they have a skewed view of sex, they may try to involve or force a younger or smaller child into sexual acts.

Some teenagers are more liable to do that. Psychologists point to a child's level of impulsiveness and ability to deal with anger and to respect boundaries.

There is no simple way parents can deal with this. Children are less innocent than in the past. So it is not surprising that some children are experimenting with sex. For parents that is a hard issue and brings up the questions of discipline, talking to children about relationships and keeping them safe – none of them easy for parents.

The lowest legal age of consent is in Nigeria where it is just 11. The highest is South Korea where it is 20.

In Israel 16.

In the United Kingdom 16.

In the USA it differs by state. In Illinois it is 17.

In Japan it can be as low as 13 if a couple is in a sincere romantic relation.

In Russia it is 16.

In Saudi Arabia there does not seem to be any particular age.

In Ireland it is 17.

Children are exploited sexually sometimes, but the data is more complicated and disturbing. The National Centre on Sexual Exploitation estimates that about one-third of all perpetrators of abuse are children under the age of 18. A film I made for Channel 4 in 1991 explored this and there has been much subsequent research. Since then there have been increased reports of younger children (age ten or younger) initiating sexual behaviour.

Apart from caning children teachers were also abusing them. A Florida educator who was recently named "Teacher of the Year" was arrested for child abuse just two days after being given the award. Caroline "Melanie" Lee, 60, allegedly asked a female student in her classroom to speak privately and hit her across the face, stated a local Schools Police report.

"Christ said suffer the little children for they shall enter the kingdom of God. Jesus called them unto him, and said, **Suffer little children** to come unto me, and forbid them not: for of such is the kingdom of God. Verily I say unto you," .... today it would be more apt to say, let the children suffer. All faiths have been guilty of covering up sexual abuse but The Catholic Church more perhaps than any other.

The report found that religious organisations often blamed the victim and discouraged external reporting. The organisation's reputation mattered more than truth and the needs of victims.

An estimated 250,000 children in England and Wales receive "supplementary schooling" or "out-of-school provision" from a faith organisation. They have no supervision or oversight in respect of child protection.

The report makes two recommendations:

i that all religious organisations should have a child protection policy and supporting procedures; and
ii that the government should legislate to amend the definition of full-time education to bring any setting that is the pupil's primary place of education within the scope of a registered school and provide Ofsted with sufficient powers to examine the quality of child protection when undertaking inspection of suspected unregistered schools.

This book has reported other people's research so far but now I dare to be original.

Chapter 13

The Parental Inferiority Complex

If I had achieved a long-held ambition of mine and become a tabloid headline writer I would head this.

Dad you're thicker than two thick planks!

Humour helps with difficult subjects – and this is a difficult one as it suggests a radical change in child-parent relationships.

In her recent biography, Jane Ridley states that George V said he was frightened of his father and had every intention of making sure his children were frightened of him.

Prince Philip criticised his son Charles often and was disappointed when he did not toughen up after being sent to Gordonstoun where Philip had thrived.

Zoe Combi, author of *Gen Z: Their Voices, Their Lives,* identifies one of the major issues dividing generations is older people dismissing the heightened feelings and reactions of younger people as disingenuous or "performative." She believes Gen Z's commitment to things such as "language purity" – there being a single right way to talk about a person or experience – is "absolutely genuine" but that does not stop it from causing dissent.

Older people are bearing the brunt of internet humour that paints them as out-of-touch Boomers with little to offer. One Combi's subjects reported her latest bugbear was being asked to put her pronouns in her email signature. "I don't mind how anyone identifies. But why should I have to write '(she/her)' on emails I send just because some 20-year-old says so?"

"I often say to the young people I work with, 'Don't hurt the importance of your message by getting angry at people for using

DOI: 10.4324/9781003165484-14

a term you find offensive,'" says Combi. "With older people who are trying, it can undermine their contribution."

The fault lines we are seeing in workplaces from funeral directors to massive media conglomerates are the same ones fracturing society. And the cracks are widening, thanks to a dangerous inability to even listen to perspectives different to one's own. Joe Twyman, co-founder of the public opinion consultancy Deltapoll, provides some context:

> "In the UK we have an older generation, which generally feels that the social changes of the past 20 or 30 years happened against their wishes and without their consent. Brexit was a symptom of this. On social media, there's a belief that everyone should be like 'me'," says Twyman. "There is a lack of understanding and acceptance of others' views, because there's a tendency in our on-demand world to choose the news and opinions we want, and cut out everything else."

History tells us nothing about the Parental Inferiority complex which I freely admit I have just invented. In this chapter, I argue that the superior techno skills of children are likely to stress out their parents. To understand the radical nature of the complex we must summons as witnesses, Winston Churchill and King George V are relevant. Both had to deal with dominating fathers.

George V's elder brother Eddy was heir to the throne when he died in 1891. His untimely death probably saved the monarchy as he had been involved in a male brothel scandal. He had been told to get engaged to Mary of Teck. When Eddy died, George was told by his father and Queen Victoria that he had to marry Mary. You did not mess with Grandma or Papa in those days of deference. He did so but as he was not the most intellectual of royals – his main hobbies were shooting birds and stamp collecting – he never analysed his motives. His younger son who became King George VI developed a stammer.

Churchill was often introspective as he suffered from what he called his black dog. I have argued elsewhere that the neglect of his parents may have caused that. Lord Randolph Churchill did not think much of his son who idolised him. Churchill wrote his only short story two years after the Second World War ended. In *The Dream*, his long-dead father appears. Churchill tries not to be frightened by this apparition which begins to cross-examine him.

What has he done with his life? When Lord Randolph died in 1895, Churchill was not a promising young man. Has he done better since then? his father demands to know.

"I was a major in the Yeomanry," Churchill replies. His father is not impressed by the middling rank. Glancing around Churchill's studio in Chartwell's fine grounds, though, he admits that his son has obviously been "able to keep himself going."

Churchill tells his father he has four children and five grandchildren. Lord Randolph then turns to the world situation. "Have there been any wars since I died?" he asks.

"They were the wars of nations, caused by demagogues and tyrants."

"Did we win?"

"Yes, we won all our wars," Churchill responds.

In telling his father that he became a major, Churchill was hiding much of the truth about his military career. By 1947, when he wrote the story, he had been a lieutenant-colonel in the army, not to mention First Lord of the Admiralty and Minister of Defence.

At one point, Lord Randolph suggests his son might have gone into politics. Churchill never reveals that he became an MP, let alone that he served as Prime Minister and steered Britain and the empire to victory in the Second World War. Interpreting Churchill's story is tempting, but not simple. The context is complex. A famous son writes a fiction, in which he conjures up his less famous father, who was usually disappointed in him. Then the son fails to tell his father all the great things he has achieved in life. Churchill's reticence obviously reveals something about his feelings; he loved his father dearly, but perhaps he did not totally trust him. Perhaps Churchill also wanted to spare his father's feelings because he had ultimately fared so much better than him. Simply Churchill did not want to make his father feel inferior.

Alfred Adler who originated the idea of an inferiority complex was at first a devoted follower of Freud. Adler believed Freud put too much emphasis on sex. He argued that the basic cause of neurosis was a sense of inferiority and that individuals who suffered from that spent their lives trying to overcome the feelings, in some cases without ever being in touch with reality (White, 1917). Freud incidentally did not have much time for Adler's ideas.

As Piaget observed, the baby is born helpless and utterly dependent on its parents. The baby has to get his or her parents' attention. Churchill was lucky in that his nurse Mrs Everest adored him and gave him the love his parents did not. His father was too obsessed with his political career; his mother with her lovers. Donald Winnicott later argued that mothers did not have to be perfect; the good enough mother could shape the child's unconscious goals. Churchill's mother only became good enough when her son was nearly 20 – probably in a lull between lovers. Adler insisted that the child strives towards rectifying that inferiority – a need to compensate for weakness by developing other strengths.

If the child gets adequate nurturing and care, she can accept his challenges, and learn that they can be overcome with hard work. Thus, the child develops "normally" and develops the "courage to be imperfect" (Lazarsfeld, 1966, pp. 163–165).

However, sometimes, the process of compensation goes wrong. The feelings of inferiority can become too intense, and the child begins to feel as though she or he has no control over his surroundings. She or he will strive very strenuously for compensation, to the point that compensation is no longer satisfactory.

The result – overcompensation, where the child's focus on meeting his goal is exaggerated and becomes pathological. For example, Adler uses the ancient Greek hero Demosthenes who had a terrible stutter but overcame it to become the "greatest orator in Greece" (p. 22).

Here, Demosthenes started off with an inferiority due to his stutter, and overcompensated by not just overcoming his stutter, but taking up a profession that would normally be impossible for a stutterer. Churchill also worried about his speaking style and sought help for it.

According to Adler (2013), the hallmark of an inferiority complex is that "persons are always striving to find a situation in which they excel" (p. 74). This drive is due to their overwhelming feelings of inferiority.

Secondary inferiority, on the other hand, is the inferiority feeling in the adult results when the child develops an exaggerated feeling of inferiority (p. 23).

Adler (2013) claimed that once a psychologist knows a person's style of life, "it is possible to predict his future sometimes just on the basis of talking to him and having him answer questions" (p. 100).

Adler, however, did not imagine that parents could feel inferior let alone threatened by their children. Today that is the case.

Teresa Correa, University Diego Portales (in Santiago, Chile), conducted in-depth interviews with 14 parent/child sets and surveyed 242 parent/child sets. She found that youth influence their parents in all technologies studied (computer, mobile internet, social networking) up to 40% of the time. The children's scores were higher compared to parents, showing that parents don't necessarily recognize the influence.

This bottom-up influence process was more likely to occur with mothers and lower socio-economic families. In low-income immigrant families too, the children act as language and culture links between the family and the new environment. Children from poorer families are more likely to receive input about technology from school and friends. So children teach their parents.

"The fact that this bottom-up technology transmission occurs more frequently among women and lower-SES families has important implications," said Correa. "Women and poor people usually lag behind in the adoption and usage of technology. Many times, they do not have the means to acquire new technologies but, most importantly, they are less likely to have the knowledge, skills, perceived competence, and positive attitudes toward digital media. These results suggest that schools in lower-income areas should be especially considered in government or foundation-led intervention programs that promote usage of digital media."

As I have introduced some invented dialogues, a small domestic might be in order:

> Dad: Photoshop. I can't do it.
>
> Daughter: Don't get stressed dad. Let me do it.
>
> Dad: I don't need your help.
>
> Daughter: Don't be a prat papa. And to help you I want you to take this.
>
> Dad: What is the Parental Inferiority Test?
>
> Daughter: Don't be scared. Be a man.

There are no right or wrong answers. The aim of the test is to give you an insight into your own technological knowledge and skills compared to your children.

1. List on a scale of 1–10 how competent you are at the following:
    Word Can you write in Word?
    Do you know how to edit in Word?
    Can you edit in Photoshop?
    Does your password include your birthday?
    Do you use
    Instagram
    What's App
    Snapchat
    Booster brain
    Google
    Booster brain doesn't exist of course,
2. Do you know when your children are using any of the above?
3. How much time a day do you spend on screen?
4. Are there conflicts in your family concerning the use of computers?
5. Do you restrict what your children have access to on devices
6. On a scale of 1–10 how much technology did you learn during the pandemic
7. Have you asked your children for help with any technology issues?
8. Are you aware that your children know more than you do about technology?
9. Are you worried that this may change your relationship to them?
10. Would you say you are as a technology skilled
    As a 3 year old
    A 6 year old
    A 12 year old
11. Do you compare your child to yourself at the same age? Wanting your child to be like you is a human trait. Did your parents want you to be a replica?

This work in progress test raises issues but it has not been validated. Nevertheless, psychologists will need to devise approaches to the study of change as the realities of techno-savvy children affect family life.

A testing interlude

Here is a game for the family to play. You sit around the table and each of you fills in a questionnaire in silence. Rank on a scale of 1–5 how the following statements apply to you.

1. I have a good sense of why I have certain feelings most of the time.
2. I have good understanding of my own emotions.
3. I really understand what I feel.
4. I always know whether or not I am happy.
5. I always know my friends' emotions from their behaviour.
6. I am a good observer of others' emotions.
7. I am sensitive to the feelings and emotions of others.
8. I have good understanding of the emotions of people around me.
9. I am able to control my temper so that I can handle difficulties rationally.
10. I am quite capable of controlling my own emotions.
11. I can always calm down quickly when I am very angry.
12. I have good control of my own emotions.

Now share your answers with others in your family and see whether they agree with your own view of yourself. You may think you have emotional intelligence but do your significant others think so too.

Chapter 14

Emotional Intelligence and Politics

Compare the ways in which Tony Blair and Gordon Brown reacted to voters. Tony Blair found it much easier to connect and his impromptu speech after the death of Princess Diana in 1997 expressed a very appropriate mix of sorrow. The royal family by comparison did not understand the emotions unleashed. Blair's colleague Gordon Brown seemed much stiffer in dealing with voters. Bill Clinton was a master of emotional connection unlike his wife who often seemed stiff.

In terms of this book the question is: is there a link between emotional intelligence and political activity?

Emotional intelligence was only "discovered" in 1985 when Leon Payne submitted a PhD thesis called *A Study of Emotion: Developing Emotional Intelligence*. Five years later, John Mayer of the University of New Hampshire and Peter Salovey of Yale University were working on ways of measuring the differences between people's abilities in the area of emotions. They found that some people were better than others at identifying their own feelings, identifying the feelings of others and solving problems involving emotional issues. The title of one of their papers was Emotional Intelligence.

Two years later Daniel Goleman, who wrote for *Psychology Today* and for the *New York Times*, discovered the 1990 article. He was planning a book on what he then called "emotional literacy" but he thought emotional intelligence would make a better title. The book stayed on the *New York Times* best-seller list for a year. Goleman made such an impact partly because he claimed emotional intelligence was the largest single predictor of success in the workplace.

DOI: 10.4324/9781003165484-15

Mayer and Salovey complained Goleman had made the definition so broad "that it no longer has any scientific meaning or utility and is no longer a clear predictor of outcome." That did not stop emotional intelligence becoming a very influential concept. Battles over its definition continue, however. Mayer, Salovey and Caruso claim emotional intelligence is "the ability to process emotional information, particularly as it involves the perception, assimilation, understanding, and management of emotion."

They have analysed EI into four components. The first is *Emotional identification, perception and expression*, which is the ability to identify emotions in faces, music and stories.

The second component is *emotional facilitation of thought*, which involves being able to use emotion in reasoning and problem-solving.

Their third component is *emotional understanding*, which is self-explanatory. Arguably this has less to do with feeling than with understanding feelings and, in some cases, simply understanding the language in which we express emotions. The fact that I can use the word "jealous" does not mean that I will handle a situation in which I feel jealous maturely.

Their fourth component is *emotional management*, understanding the implications of social acts on emotions and the regulation of emotion in self and others. Some of this seems to be related to the capacity to stand back and see how what we do can affect others. This is not just an emotional skill but also an intellectual one. I can learn, for example, that it is wiser to pause if I am in the middle of a domestic row rather than immediately responding by screaming "You bastard" if I discover my partner has been having an affair with her next door.

One omission is that none of these authors discusses the intensity of feelings which often drive protest.

The Israeli psychologist Reuven Bar-On (2006) developed one of the first measures that used the term Emotion Quotient, which, of course, echoes IQ or Intelligence Quotient. Bar-On claims emotional intelligence develops over time and can be improved through training, programming and therapy.

How does this affect political attitudes?

Research from Belgium suggests that deficits in emotion understanding and emotion management are related to right-wing and prejudiced attitudes. The study has been published in the journal *Emotion*.

"I have a lifelong interest in political psychology and in political ideology in particular. The observation that left-wing and right-wing adherents tend to differ on so many psychological characteristics is amazing," said Alain Van Hiel, a professor at the University of Ghent.

"Many scholars have investigated the cognitive basis of ideology in general, and right-wing ideological attitudes in particular. In the present study, we wanted to investigate if a similar relationship would exist for emotional abilities."

In two studies, the researchers assessed the emotional abilities and political ideology of 983 Belgian undergraduate students. The second study also examined the participants' cognitive ability. Emotional ability was measured with three tests: the Situational Test of Emotional Understanding, the Situational Test of Emotion Management and the Geneva Emotion Recognition Test.

The researchers found that individuals with weaker emotional abilities – particularly emotional understanding and management – tended to score higher on a measure of right-wing authoritarianism and social dominance orientation.

Right-wing authoritarianism is a personality trait that describes the tendency to submit to political authority and be hostile towards other groups, while social dominance orientation is a measure of a person's preference for inequality among social groups.

"The results of this study were univocal. People who endorse authority and strong leaders and who do not mind inequality – the two basic dimensions underlying right-wing political ideology – show lower levels of emotional abilities," Van Hiel told PsyPost.

Those with lower emotional and cognitive abilities were also more likely to agree with blatantly prejudiced statements such as "The White race is superior to all other races."

The researchers controlled for age, sex and education level. But like all research, the study includes some limitations. The study only collected correlational data, preventing inferences of causality from being made.

"Of course, caution should be exercised in the interpretation of such results," Van Hiel said. "One cannot discredit any ideology on the basis of such results as those presently obtained.

Only in a distant future we will be able to look back upon our times, and then we can maybe judge which ideologies were the best. Cognitively and emotionally smart people can make wrong decisions as well."

"The results have been obtained in one particular context. Would similar results be obtained in other contexts besides in a Western country with a long-standing stable democracy? Whether these tendencies are universal, or limited to particular contexts, is very intriguing."

Self-control, one aspect of emotional intelligence, is particularly important in many ways and it predicts achievement in children. A particularly powerful study tested school-aged children on self-control and conducted follow-up studies on them in their 30s. Self-control predicted success better than IQ, socio-economic status and family environment. Children who scored high on self-control were also healthier, made more money and were less likely to have criminal records or trouble with alcohol.

John Gottman, in *Raising an Emotionally Intelligent Child,* argues parents can help children become aware of their emotions early in life by recognizing emotions as they arise. If Johnny knocks down his blocks when he is told it's time for bed, you can say, "I know you are angry, but if you pick up the blocks we'll play with them again tomorrow." When children test boundaries, according to Gottman, it's an opportunity to create an "intimate moment of learning." So if Debbie is mad at her friend, the emotionally wise parent says, "Oh, you don't really hate Mary." Gottman suggests instead that you validate her feelings. Perhaps you could say something like "You seem really mad, what happened?"

There seem to be no studies of how effective such coaching may be but there is certainly an appetite for it as the success of how to parent shows like Supernanny on British TV shows. Supernanny observes the family and gives desperate mum and dad into parents who can help their children cope with their feelings and frustrations. Being able to express these is important. Children who learn about feelings, how to express them and control them, are likely to function better than children who are the opposite – and that is not just a common sense guess.

Gottman observed how different parents respond to their children's emotions. He found four possible ways.

1. Dismissing parents see children's emotions as unimportant and attempt to eliminate them quickly, often through the use of distraction.
2. Disapproving parents see negative emotions as something to be squashed, usually through punishment.
3. Laissez-faire parents accept all emotions from child but fail to help her or him solve problems or put limits on appropriate behaviours.
4. Gottman also described a group of parents as "emotion coaching parents." They value negative emotions, are not impatient with a child's expression of them, and use emotional experience as an opportunity for bonding by offering guidance through labelling emotions and problem-solving the issue at hand.

Gottman offered a sensible but obvious five-step guide for parents to help parents develop their child's emotional development.

Step 1: Be aware of your child's emotions.
Parents who emotion coach are aware of their own feelings and sensitive to their children's emotions. They respond before their children become dramatic in their emotional expression for the feelings to be acknowledged.

Step 2: See emotions as an opportunity for connection and teaching.
Children's emotions are not an inconvenience or a challenge. They are an opportunity to connect with children and coach them through a challenging feeling.

Step 3: Listen and validate the feelings.
Give children full attention while you listen to their emotional expression. Reflect back on what you hear, thus telling your child you understand what they are seeing and experiencing.

Step 4: Label their emotions.
Help your child develop an awareness of and vocabulary for their emotional expression.

Step 5: Help your child problem-solve with limits.
All emotions are acceptable, but all behaviours are not. Help your child cope with his or her emotions by developing problem-solving skills. Limit the expression to appropriate behaviours.

Children of parents who emotionally coach are physically healthier, do better in school and get along better with friends. Emotion coaching parents followed five basic steps to help their children with emotions. Sometimes this can take a great deal of time.

Gottman found no parents were perfect and always managed to react in such an understanding way. The best only managed to do it about a quarter of the time. He concluded there was no need for parents to feel guilty as no parent is emotionally perfect.

Chapter 15

Mental Health and Technology

Officer Krupsky we're down on our knees

The great song in West Side Story emphasises the young New York gangs could all do with some time on the couch.

Mark Zuckerberg's mother is a psychiatrist herself. It could be argued her son has made sure her profession keeps busy.

Psychiatry was in its infancy during the Industrial Revolution in the 19th century and studies did not focus much on the mental health effects of the development of factories though Marx argued workers suffered from alienation. The 1870s onwards saw huge technological changes – electrification, the telephone, the motor car, and the first aeroplanes. Psychiatry, however, did not concentrate on how the rush of the modern affected mental health very much. Initially during the 1914–1919 war, most psychiatrists did not take how shell shock crippled many soldiers seriously.

In 2021, the mental health issues have some similarities. The world is changing and we have to adapt. Evidence from two countries shows that is not easy.

Some of the most powerful arguments against Facebook come from Nigeria where Larshmi has written on relevance of Facebook Addiction which he sees as part of Internet Spectrum Addiction Disorder. Many young adults in Nigeria are undiscerning users of Social network sites which they use too much or are already entrapped in the "web" of addictions. Larshmi (2011) surveyed the level of addiction to Facebook among selected Nigerian University undergraduates and used the Facebook Addiction Symptoms Scale (FASS). He described the disorder:

DOI: 10.4324/9781003165484-16

> The first thing you do in the morning is to check your Facebook account. – Whenever you are not online, you day-dream of the comments and status updates that have been received. – You spend hours or waste a lot of precious time on Facebook. – Your day ends only after a last check of your Facebook account and wishing everyone "good night" as status update. It showed many undergraduates access Facebook account every passing hour, every two hours and every day. Although the study observed low level of addiction, this result may be due to the low level of internet access generally in Nigeria. The study therefore suggests that stake holders must do something to prevent rampant Facebook addiction in particular and internet addiction in general among Nigerian youths.

In Nigeria, most university undergraduates like to stay up-to-date and what makes this increasingly alarming is that students can access their Facebook accounts on their mobile phones. Often, when lectures are going on, students still find time to chat with friends online or respond to Facebook notifications which takes their minds off their academic work.

A 2021 study in Switzerland looked at students in two undergraduate programs at the time of the COVID-19 crisis. At this point, the university had been under lockdown for about two weeks. The Swiss government had further implemented a number of social distancing measures and individuals had to stay at home. The study compared measures on social networks and mental health to (i) those of the same students seven months earlier (prior to the COVID-19 outbreak).

Most students remained well-integrated after two weeks of physical distancing and when face-to-face interaction was impossible, digital communication was very common. However, the increasing number of isolated individuals suggested that some individuals might struggle more. Students were on average more depressed, slightly more anxious, more stressed and felt more lonely than half a year earlier. While measures of mental health suggest a decline, some students reported that the crisis situation affected their lives positively. They could not suffer from Fear of Missing Out (FOMO) syndrome when they could not go to any gig or club. Competition among the students also became less intense.

Women were more likely to be affected negatively by the situation but often they could rely on stronger support networks potentially helping them to cope. Decline in mental health measures was associated with more worries about one's family and friends, more worries about the future career, being faced with problems usually suppressed, living alone and less contact and support from the personal network.

A study in *Pediatrics* found that routinely using social media can enhance "communication, social connection, and even technical skills." The downside, however, is considerable, as it can also fuel feelings of loneliness, anxiety and depression. Some of the biggest problems include:

- Cyberbullying. Children and teens who spend a lot of time online may experience cyberbullying. This pervasive form of bullying never stops, and adolescents may receive cruel or hurtful messages whenever they are online. That can trigger anxiety, depression, behavioural issues, low self-esteem or even suicidal thoughts.
- Phone addiction. Almost half of the teenagers surveyed in the Digital Wellbeing 2020 study believe they are addicted to their smartphones. Over 50% also felt that their lives (in terms of diet, sleep, exercise and schoolwork) were negatively impacted by their relationship with technology.
- Increased anxiety and depression. The more time kids spend on their screens, the more anxious they become. Teens who spend over three hours a day on social media are more likely to internalize their problems, increasing the risk of depression, anxiety and the FOMO.
- Disordered sleep. Using phones in bed disrupts sleep, making it difficult to relax, fall asleep and stay asleep. Kids who don't sleep well are more likely to have mental health problems such as depression, impulsive behaviour, anxiety and even lower scores on cognitive tests.

Body image

Prince Diana suffered from anorexia and bulimia. So do many teenagers who worry about how attractive they look. Social media exposes them to nasty messages sometimes which also affect how well they feel about themselves. This fear has gone East. Ganesan et al (2018) showed that body image dissatisfaction was there in 77.6% of the adolescents. This was similar to a study done by Sasi and Maran in Chennai among adolescents above 12 years of age which showed a prevalence of 81%.

Our study also showed that 23% of the underweight people were satisfied with their BMI, and among those who were dissatisfied 7.4% wanted to reduce their weight further. The study also showed that the proportion of girls having body image dissatisfaction, who belonged to class I socio-economic status, is slightly higher than other classes. Increased socio-cultural pressure, depression and higher BMI had significant association with body image dissatisfaction.

A total of 64.8% of the college students had tried at least one weight control measure in the past one year. It also showed that girls who were dissatisfied with their appearance tend to do more weight control measures. Most cited improving the appearance and to look better in clothes as main reasons for going in for weight control measures. This was also found similar to other studies which showed that appearance was a major motivation for dieting practices. Social media allows us to compare ourselves against others and that makes many teenagers unhappy.

Profit over safety

Frances Haugen, who had worked for Facebook, pitched the social network into crisis. She told American senators that the Silicon Valley company repeatedly prioritised "profit over safety," money over mental health.

Facebook has argued that it is trying, through projects such as Instagram Kids, to make it safer for children to take their first steps online. But Haugen suggested that Facebook viewed younger users as an untapped source of growth and studied ways to hook a new generation of users. "Facebook's own research says it is not just [that] Instagram is dangerous for teenagers, that it harms teenagers, it's that it is distinctly worse than other forms of social media," Haugen told the television programme 60 Minutes. After Joe Biden was elected, Haugen alleged, Facebook executives decided it could "get rid of civic integrity now." That was the moment she made her mind up; she could not "trust that they're willing to actually invest what needs to be invested to keep Facebook from being dangerous." The detail of her accusations come later in the chapter.

Lack of concentration

Heavy social media users perform worse on cognitive tests, especially those that require their attention and ability to multitask. They need more effort to remain focused and not get distracted. Heavy social media users become less able to ignore distraction. Neuroimaging suggests this shrinks parts of the brain associated with maintaining attention.

Social media provides immediate rewards in the form of a dopamine release (the happy hormone) every time you post or get a notification from the app. This constant barrage of shallow rewards rewires the brain to want more of what caused that dopamine release, which contributes to social media addiction. Brain scans of heavy social media users look very similar to those addicted to drugs or gambling.

Heavy social media use is also linked with memory deficits. Its central feature, the sharing and storing of your experiences, may actually be altering which memories you keep and which ones you don't. In one study, subjects were asked to record an experience using their notes or social media, and other groups were asked to simply experience the event without recording it. At the end of the study, those who had recorded or shared the event performed worse and showed more of a memory deficit than those who experienced the event without recording it. Externalizing an experience worsened memory because their brain received the message that it didn't need to hold onto information that was stored elsewhere. Consequently, not only did the individuals lose some memory of their original experience, but they might also experience longer term deficits in the size and function of their brains.

One dramatic study even claims one child in three enters school developmentally delayed (HELP EDI Maps 2014). Against these seeming Luddites, ready to punch back, in the blue corner, the techno-lovers argue our digital age is a wonder. Children get cascades of information and the chance to acquire new skills. The digital world is their oyster.

The Commissioner's call to arms

In her last annual report on the state of children's mental health services in England, the Children's Commissioner said she had heard a "torrent of stories" from children about needing mental health services that weren't there for them. She acknowledged there had been "an unprecedented number of Government initiatives, a Green Paper, a White Paper and other commitments on children's mental health. If we look solely at how services have expanded, we can see a significant improvement from a very poor starting position. However, if we look at this in terms of the underlying needs of children, the improvements seem far more modest." Children were not being offered the services they needed and "hundreds of thousands of children are being left without help as a result."

Kelly and Sacker (Lancet 2018) found a link between social media use and depressive symptoms and that this was stronger for girls than for boys. The *UK Household Longitudinal Study* showed that girls with greater social media use at the start of adolescence had poorer mental well-being several years on.

Their results and those of others highlight the complexity of mechanisms involved. Given the short- and long-term implications of having poor mental health, improving our understanding of underlying processes could help identify opportunities for interventions that would limit damage.

The whistle-blower – Francis Haugen again

Haugen worked for nearly two years at Facebook, where she was the lead product manager on the civic-integrity team. "I came to realize the devastating truth. Almost no one outside of Facebook knows what happens inside of Facebook," she told senators in Washington. "The company intentionally hides vital information from the public, from the U.S. government, and from governments around the world." She added, "Facebook wants you to believe that the problems we are talking about are unsolvable. They want you to believe in false choices. They want you to believe that you must choose between a Facebook full of divisive and extreme content or losing one of the most important values our country was founded upon, free speech .... That to be able to share fun photos of your kids with old friends you must also be inundated with anger-driven virality. They want you to believe that this is just part of the deal. I am here today to tell you that that's not true."

Haugen also told 60 Minutes that Facebook's own research showed divisive content was more engaging. "Facebook has realised that if they change the algorithm to be safer, people will spend less time on the site, they'll click on less ads, they'll make less money," she said, and that after the 2020 US election the company chose to "prioritise growth over safety." The company has denied the allegations, saying it continues to improve its algorithms to reduce "clickbait."

But many politicians in the United States and Europe believe self-regulation does not go far enough. Mark Zuckerberg responded that Haugen's claims "don't make sense," adding that "at the heart of these accusations is this idea that we prioritize profit over safety and well-being. That's just not true."

The research also indicates that, even as Instagram makes teenagers unhappy or ill, they find it difficult to stop using the app. What others call "addiction," Haugen said, Facebook calls "problematic use." She also noted that adolescents often create secret Instagram accounts, which they hide from their parents and from which the company benefits, because they boost advertising revenue.

About an hour into Haugen's Senate appearance, Facebook's policy communications director, Andy Stone, in an apparent effort to blunt her testimony, took to Twitter, writing that she was talking about research that she had not conducted herself and had "no direct knowledge of." In her testimony, Haugen acknowledged that she did not work directly on the Instagram research and was relying on the analyses of those who did.

Facebook desperately wants to avoid regulation, critics say, so it pours millions into lobbying efforts while fighting legal battles around the world against attempts to rein in its power. In April 2018, during nearly five hours of questioning by 44 US senators, Zuckerberg repeated apologies he previously made for a range of problems that have beset Facebook, from a lack of data protection to Russian agents using Facebook to influence US elections.

But the 33-year-old internet mogul managed to deflect any specific promises to support any congressional regulation of the world's largest social media network and other US internet companies.

"I'll have my team follow up with you so that way we can have this discussion across the different categories where I think this discussion needs to happen," Zuckerberg told a joint hearing by the US Senate's Commerce and Judiciary committees, when asked what regulations he thought were necessary.

A growing number of data privacy laws in states such as California seek to limit the company's ability to harvest the user data it relies on to sell targeted ads.

Under its new chair, Lina Khan, the Federal Trade Commission, in August refiled an antitrust lawsuit against Facebook that claimed the company "resorted to an illegal buy-or-bury scheme to maintain its dominance." Last month, DC Attorney General Karl Racine added Mark Zuckerberg to a privacy lawsuit that alleges Facebook misled consumers and allowed a third party to obtain sensitive data for tens of millions of users.

Legislation aimed at restricting what platforms can do with users' data are especially important for Facebook, researchers say, because the company has a business that tracks users' activity, sucks up their data and uses it to sell targeted ads. Critics say this ad revenue model gives the company an incentive to keep users on its platform through promoting high-engagement posts, which often means inflammatory and divisive content. Users like controversy. Privacy laws that put restrictions on Facebook's brand of surveillance capitalism could have the dual effect of limiting discriminatory ad practices and preventing misinformation from being promoted to users. Before any attempt to regulate Facebook, many experts say we need legislation forcing the company to disclose how its algorithms actually work. Facebook has continuously tried to evade outside efforts to show how their algorithms function. Earlier this year the company forced the shutdown of two research projects studying how its platforms promote content, one from New York University and the other from the German organization Algorithm Watch.

Both incidents highlighted what researchers say is a fundamental issue of any attempt to regulate the company: a stifling lack of transparency, where it appears even Facebook is unclear on how its algorithms work. Researchers and lawmakers are calling for the company to finally let regulators take a look at the inner workings.

One telling Facebook experiment showed that when company researchers created a fake profile named "Carol Smith" and made it follow conservative accounts such as Fox News and Donald Trump, they found that within two days the algorithms suggested Carol join QAnon groups. The experiment was one of many tests in recent years that Facebook conducted to understand the full impact of its algorithms, and one that didn't come to light until it was revealed in the leaked documents.

"We can't rely on whistle-blowers. It's fantastic that they're there. It's fantastic that they have the courage to do something like this, but this is not enough," said Matthias Spiel Kamp, the founder and executive director of Algorithm Watch. "It's not a regulatory model to just wait until some whistle-blower tells us what is going on behind the scenes. We need more access."

Additional pressure has come as the European Parliament is debating legislation intended to prohibit platforms such as Facebook from exploiting users' data and engaging in unfair business practices. And, in the United Kingdom, a member of Parliament, Damian Collins, is shepherding through a new online-safety bill.

None of this necessarily means, of course, that Facebook will be reformed in any meaningful way. As Senator Amy Klobuchar told Haugen, "I think the time has come for action. And I think you are the catalyst for that action. You have said privacy legislation is not enough. I completely agree with you. But I think, you know, we have not done anything to update our privacy laws in this country, our federal privacy laws – nothing, zilch – in any major way. Why? Because there are lobbyists around every single corner of this building that have been hired by the tech industry. We have done nothing when it comes to making the algorithms more transparent .... Why? Because Facebook and the other tech companies are throwing a bunch of money around this town and people are listening to them."

The former British Deputy Prime Minister Nick Clegg told CNN that the company might accept more regulations. That would be a good thing, because Haugen could not have been clearer when she warned that, if Facebook continues to do business as usual, "the divisive and extremist behaviours we see today are only the beginning" of the story. "No one," she said, "wants to read the end of it."

Large companies usually have health departments. Facebook with its changes of name suggests the company and its founder have identity issues – and so need a potful of therapists. Headed perhaps by Zuckerberg's mother.

Chapter 16

The Typical Child 2046

I have learned among much else what I do not know and also what psychologists do not know. Ignorance if we admit it is not necessarily bad. But we have to face it. I do not apologise for raising so many questions, but this is a moment of crisis and a moment of change.

The questions need a mix of approaches and methods. I have outlined them boldly but they are all complicated because of the mix of

History
Situation
Personality

So what follows is simplification but we need to study at least:

> What motivates young people to become politically active?. Protest has its limits. What happens to the children who become very involved in school councils and children's parliaments? Does it make them become councillors and candidates?

The personality of activists also needs study. There are those who feel strongly but do not take much action. What makes the difference?

What will be the impact when the tech-savvy young of today become parents themselves? Will they know more or less than their offspring and how will that affect them?

How do we encourage the young to vote?

DOI: 10.4324/9781003165484-17

How do we force techno giants to acknowledge the problems they cause and put profits not always first?

How do we develop the art of listening to children?

How can the problems caused by the children knowing more than parents be resolved?

Let us finish by imagining twenty years from now.

Where the U.S.A started the Peace Corps in the 1960s, there is now a Tree Corps who spend time reforesting. The petrol and diesel car is now an antique. Planes have become more energy efficient but airfares are more expensive discouraging unnecessary travel. Crucially we have learned to mollycoddle ourselves less so we put up with the cold more than we did. Sales of coats, scarves and woolly hats have boomed.

There is a large group of politicians who are under 30 years old and who challenge the established order not as protesters but as active politicians. They are more willing to use traditional political tactics to persuade, even force, oil companies and other vested interests to abandon old practices. What is hard to predict is the way in which new technologies have made being green more practical.

I will end with another fancy. Three professors are meeting. One is dead – Professor Freud – one is Professor Jehovah who is for some the ultimate reality but for others a myth. The third is Professor Marcus Rashford. He and Greta Thunberg married in the marriage of the century demoting the now 80-year-old wedding of Prince Charles and Princess Diana to the tatters of history.

Professor Freud: What is the problem now?

Professor Marcus Rashford: I know things are better but there is still so much to do.

Professor Jehovah: I remember the feeling. I created heaven and earth in six days and then realised it was not the end of my labours because I gave the children of Israel free will.

Professor Freud: As Voltaire said at the end of Candide we must cultivate our garden – and keep on cultivating.

Professor Rashford: As long as we don't eat meat!

The increasing power of children and young people must give us hope that human beings will weed out at least most of the poisons that threaten us.

References

Adler, A. (1979). *Superiority and Social Interest*. New York: W.W Norton.

Adler, A. (2013). *The Practice and Theory of Individual Psychology*. Santa Fe: Martino Fine Books.

Alabi, O. F. (2013). A survey of Facebook addiction level among selected Nigerian university undergraduates. *New Media and Mass Communication*, *10*(2012), 70–80.

Alford, J. R., Funk, C. L., and Hibbing, J. R. (2005). Are political orientations genetically transmitted? *The American Political Science Review*, *99*, 153–167. 10.1017/S0003055405051579

American Academy of Paediatrics. (2016). Media and young minds. *Pediatrics*. 10.1542/peds.2016-2591

Amnesty. (June 2021). In the Name of National Security paper. Amnesty International London.

Andreassen, C. S., Griffiths, M. D., Gjertsen, S. R., Krossbakken, E., Kvam, S., and Pallesen, S. (2013). The relationships between behavioral addictions and the five-factor model of personality. *Journal of Behavioral Addictions*, *2*(2), 90–99.

Austin, E. J., Saklofske, D. H., and Egan, V. (2005). Personality, well-being and health correlates of trait emotional intelligence. *Personality and Individual Differences*, *38*(3), 547–558.

Auxier, B., and Anderson, M. (2021). *Social Media Use in 2021*. Washington: Pew Research Centre.

Bányai, F., Zsila, Á., Király, O., Maraz, A., Elekes, Z., Griffiths, M. D., Andreassen, C. S., and Demetrovics, Z. (2017). Problematic social media use: Results from a large-scale nationally representative adolescent sample. *PLoS ONE*, *12*(1).

Bayer, P., Ferreira, F., and McMillan, R. (2007). A unified framework for measuring preferences for schools and neighborhoods. *Journal of Political Economy*, *115*, 588–638.

Bee, H. L. (1994). *Lifespan Development*. New York: HarperCollins College Publishers.

Beranuy, M., Oberst, U., Carbonell, X., and Chamarro, A. (2009). Problematic internet and mobile phone use and clinical symptoms in college students: The role of emotional intelligence. *Computers in Human Behavior*, *25*(5), 1182–1187. 10.1016/j.chb.2009.03.001

Betancourt, T. S., Brennan, R. T., and Thomson, D. (2019). Stigma and acceptance of Sierra Leone's child soldiers: A prospective longitudinal study of adult mental health and social functioning. *Journal of the American Academy of Child and Adolescent Psychiatry*, *59* (6), 715–726.

Bettelheim, B. (1991). *The Uses of Enchantment*. Harmondsworth: Penguin.

Binet, A., and Simon, T. (2015). The Development of Intelligence in Children. Palala Press: New York.

Blake, W.(1838). *Songs of Innocence and Experience*.Wilder publications Saint Paul Minnesota. Republished (2007). Tate Publications, London.

Bleakley, A., Ellithorpe, M., and Romer, D. (2016). *The Role of Parents in Problematic Internet Use among US Adolescents*. Washington: Annenberg Public Policy Centre.

Bonanno, G., Galea, S., Bucciarelli, A., and Vladhow, D. (October 2007). What predicts psychological resilience after disaster? The role of demographics, resources, and life stress. *Journal of Consulting and Clinical Psychology*, *75*, 671–682.

Bouchard, T. J., and McGue, M. (2003). Genetic and environmental influences on human psychological differences. *Journal of Neurobiology*, 54, 4–45. 10.1002/neu.10160

Bowlby, J. (1997). *Attachment and Love*. London: Pimlico.

Bowlby J., and Ainsworth M. (1965). *Attachment and the Growth of Love*. Harmondsworth: Penguin.

Brad, V. P., and Hatemi, P. K. (2011). Disentangling the importance of psychological predispositions and social constructions in the organization of American political ideology. *Political Psychology*, *3*(3), 375–393.

Bradmetz, J. (1998). Piaget et les chimères conceptuelles: éloge du constructivisme. *Bulletin de psychologie*, *51*(3), P61–81.

Bratsberg, B., and Rogeberg, O. Flynn effect and its reversal are both environmentally caused. *Proceedings of the National Academy of Sciences*, *115*(26), 6674–6678. 10.1073/pnas.1718793115

Brewin, C. (2009). Memory processes in post-traumatic stress disorder. *International Review of Psychiatry*, *47*(7), 159–163.

Britain Thinks Survey xxx The Kids are Alright: How do Gen Z feel about the nation, their prospects (and their parents)?

Buckstone, J. B. (1853). *Harlequin and The Three Bears; or, Little Silver Hair and the Fairies in Aunt Mavor's Nursery Tales*. London: George Routledge and Co.

Cammaerts, B., Bruter, M., Banaji, S., Harrison, S., and Anstead, N. (2014). The myth of youth apathy young Europeans' critical attitudes toward democratic life. *American Behavioral Science*, *58*, 645–664. 10.1177/0002764213515992

Campbell, A., Converse, P. E., Miller, W. E., and Stokes, D. E. (1960). *The American Voter*. New York: John Wiley.

Caplan, S. E. (2003). Preference for online social interaction: A theory of problematic internet use and psychosocial well-being. *Communication Research*, *30*(6): 625–648.

Casanova, G. (2002). *A History of My Life*. London: Penguin.

Catani, C., Jacob, N. et al. (2008). Family violence, war, and natural disasters: A study of the effect of extreme stress on children's mental health in Sri Lanka. *BMC Psychiatry*, *8*, 33.

Churchill, W. (1947). *The Dream* originally unpublished MS referred to in Cohen D Churchill and Attlee (2019) Biteback, London.

Cohen, D. (1978). Interview with Julian Stanley, New Scientist p. 328–9 August 3rd.

Coalition to Stop the Use of Child Soldiers. (2008). Coalition to Stop the Use of Child Soldiers. London, United Kingdom.

Cohen, D. (1983). *Piaget – Critique and Reassessment*. London: Croom Helm.

Cohn Bendit, D. (2010). *Helden Haft*. Frankfurt.

Colby, A., Kohlberg, L., Gibbs, J., and Lieberman, M. (1983). A longitudinal study of moral judgment. *Monographs of the Society for Research in Child Development*. Chicago: University of Chicago Press.

Cook, A., Blaustein, M., Spinazzola, J., and van der Kolk, B. (2003). Complex trauma in children and adolescents. (White paper from the National Child Traumatic Stress Network Complex Trauma Task Force). Los Angeles: National Center for Child Traumatic Stress.

Correa, T. (2013). Bottom-up technology transmission within families: Exploring how youths influence their parents' digital media use with dyadic data. *Journal of Communication*. 10.1111/jcom.12067

Cundall, J. (1995). *Goldilocks and the three* bears Kingfisher London.

Curtice, J., and Ormston, R. (2015). British Social Survey National Centre for Social Research London, available online at: www.bsa.natcen.ac.uk

Dahl, R. A. (1973). *Polyarchy: Participation and Opposition*. New Haven, CT: Yale University Press.

De, Zousa (2021). First message as Children's Commissioner; office of the Children's Commissioner; London.

Defoe, D. (2003). *A Journal of the Plague Year*. London: Penguin Classics.

Dinas, E. (2013). Why does the apple fall far from the tree? Early Political socialisation prompts parents child dissimilarity. *British Journal of Political Science*, *44*(4), 827–852. https://doi.org/10.1017/S0007123413000033

Diseth, A. (December 2015). The advantages of task-based and other-based achievement goals as standards of competence. *International Journal of Educational Research*, 72(1). 10.1016/j.ijer.2015.04.011

Dundes, A. (1991). Bruno Bettelheim's uses of enchantment and abuses of scholarship. *Journal of American Folklore, 104.411* (Winter 1991), 74–83.

Duras, M. (1960). *Hiroshima Mon Amour*. Paris: Gallimard.

Easton, D., Dennis, J., and Easton, S. (1969). *Children in the Political System: Origins of Political Legitimacy*. New York: McGraw-Hill.

Eckstein, K., Noack, P., and Gniewosz, B. (2012). Attitudes toward political engagement and willingness to participate in politics: Trajectories throughout adolescence. *Journal of Adolescence*, *35*, 485–495. 10.1016/j.adolescence.2011.07.002

Ekström, M., and Shehata, A. (2018). Social media, porous boundaries, and the development of online political engagement among young citizens. *New Media Society*, *20*, 740–759. 10.1177/1461444816670325

Eliot, T. S. (2011). *The Wasteland*. London: Faber and Faber.

Espinar-Ruiz, E., and Gonzalez-Rio, M. J. (2015). Spanish young people's internet use and political practices. *Convergencia*, *22*, 13–38.

Festinger, L. (1957). *A Theory of Cognitive Dissonance*. Stanford: Stanford University Press.

Fiske, D. W. (1949). Consistency of the factorial structures of personality ratings from different sources. *The Journal of Abnormal and Social Psychology*, *44*(3), 329–344. 10.1037/h0057198

Flanagan, C. A. (2013). *Teenage Citizens: The Political Theories of the Young*. Cambridge, MA: Harvard University Press. 10.4159/harvard.9780674067233

Freud, S. (1913). On the Occurrence of Dreans in Fairy Tales. Standard of the Complete Works of Sigmund Freud vol 24 in the Standard Edition the Collected Works of Sigmund Freud. Hogarth Press: London.

Freud, S. (1996). *The Interpretation of Dreams*. London: Penguin.

Galton, F. (2018). *On Hereditary Genius*. New York: Palala Press.

Ganesan, Y., Talwar, P., and Norsiah Fauzan Oon, Y. B. (2018). A study on stress level and coping strategies among undergraduate students. *Journal of Cognitive Sciences and Human Development*, *3*(2). 10.33736/jcshd.787.2018

García-Albacete, G. M. (2014). *Young People's Political Participation in Western Europe: Continuity or Generational Change?* Basingstoke: Palgrave Macmillan. 10.1057/9781137341310

Gentry, B. (2018). *Why Youth Vote*. Frankfurt: Springer.

Getzels, J. W., and Jackson, P. W. (1962). *Creativity and Intelligence: Explorations with Gifted Students*. Wiley.

Gilligan, C. (1977). In a different voice: Women's conceptions of self and of morality. *Harvard Educational Review*, *47*(4), 481–517.

Global Youth Survey. (2021). published by the United Nations, New York.

Goldberg, L. R. (1990). An alternative "description of personality": The Big-Five factor structure. *Journal of Personality and Social Psychology*, *59*(6), 1216–1229. 10.1037/0022-3514.59.6.1216

Goleman, D. (1995). *Emotional Intelligence*. London: Bloomsbury.

Gopal, A. (2015). *No Good Men Among the Living*. New York: Henry Holt and Co.

Gottman, J., and Joan De Claire. (1998). *Raising an Emotionally Intelligent Child*. Englewood Cliffs: Prentice Hall.

Griffiths, M. D. (1998). Internet addiction: Does it really exist? In J. Gackenbach (ed), *Psychology and the Internet*, pp. 61–75. New York: Academic Press.

Griffiths, M. D., and Hunt, N. (1998). Dependence on Computer games by adolescents. *Psychological Reports*, *82*, 475–480.

Hansard. (2019). Audit of Political Engagement House of Commons London.

Harlacher T., Okot F., Obonyo M., and Atkinson R. R. (2006). *Traditional Ways of Coping in Acholi: Cultural Provisions for Reconciliation and Healing from War*. Kampala: Intersoft Business Services.

Hatemi, P. K., Gillespie, N. A., Eaves, L. J., Maher, B. S., Webb, B. T., Heath, A. C. (2011). A genome-wide analysis of liberal and conservative political attitudes. *Journal Politics*, *73*, 271–285. 10.1017/S002238161 0001015

Heissen, R. K., Glass, C. R., and Knight, L. A. (1987). Assessing computer anxiety development and validation of the computer anxiety rating scale. *Computers in Human Behaviour*, *3*, 49–59.

HELP EDI Maps. (2014). 10 Reasons Why Handheld Devices Should Be Banned for Children Under the Age of 12 December 18, 2014. http://www.huffingtonpost.com/cris-rowan/10-reasons-why-handheld-devices-should-be-banned_b_4899218.html?ncid=fcbklnkushpmg00000063

Henn, M., and Foard, N. (2013). Social differentiation in young people's political participation: the impact of social and educational factors on youth political engagement in Britain. *Journal of Youth Studies*, *65*(1), 360–380. https://doi.org/10.1080/13676261.2013.830704

Hitchens, C. (2008). Baby P The Mail on Sunday 16.11.

Hooghe, M., and Stolle, D. (2003). Age matters: Life-cycle and cohort differences in the socialisation effect of voluntary participation. *European Political Science*, *2*, 49–56. 10.1057/eps.2003.19

Hooghe, M., and Stolle, D. (2003). *Generating Social Capital: Civil Society and Institutions in Comparative Perspective*. London: Palgrave. 10.1057/9781403979544

Hudson, L. (1967). *Contrary Imaginations*. Harmondsworth: Penguin.

International Labour Organisation. (2020). *Estimates of Child Labour*. Geneva: ILO.

Jacob, N. et al. (2008). Family violence, war, and natural disasters: A study of the effect of extreme stress on children's mental health in Sri Lanka. *BMC Psychiatry*, *8*, 33.

Jay, A. (2021). *Independent Inquiry into Child Sexual Abuse*. HMSO London.

Jennings, W. S., and Twyman (October 2016). The dimensions and impact of political discontent in Britain. *Parliamentary Affairs*, *69*(4), 876–900. 10.1093/pa/gsv067

John, O. P. (1990). The Big Five Factor Taxonomy. In L. Pervin (ed) *Handbook of Theory and Research*. New York: Guildford Press New York.

Jung, C. (1960). Man and his Symbols London. New York, NY: Doubleday.

Jung, C. (1964). *Shambala*. Cambridge: Cambridge University Press.

Kelly, Y., and Sacker, A. (2018). Social media use and adolescent mental health: Findings from the UK millennium cohort study. *The Lancet*, *393*, 59–68.

King, L. A., King, D. W., Fairbank, J. A., Keane, T. M., and Adams, G. A. (1998). Resilience–recovery factors in post-traumatic stress disorder among female and male Vietnam veterans: Hardiness, postwar social support, and additional stressful life events. *Journal of Personality and Social Psychology*, *74*, 420–434 10.1037/0022-3514.74.2.420

Kiousis, S., and McDevitt, M. (2008). Agenda setting in civic development effects of curricula and issue importance on Youth Voter Turnout. *Communication Research*, *35*, 481–502.

Klasen, F., Oettingen, G., Daniels, J., Post, M., Catrin, H., and Hubertus, A.(July–August 2010). Posttraumatic resilience in former Ugandan child soldiers. *Child Development*, *81*(4), 1096–1113. 10.1111/j.1467-8624.2010.01456.x

Kobasa, S. C., Maddi, S. R., and Kahn, S. (January 1982). Hardiness and health: A prospective study. *Journal of Personality and Social Psychology*, *42*(1), 168–177. 10.1037//0022-3514.42.1.168

Kohlberg, L. (1958). The Development of Modes of Thinking and Choices in Years 10 to 16. Ph. D. Dissertation, University of Chicago.

Kohlberg, L. (1984). *The Psychology of Moral Development: The Nature and Validity of Moral Stages (Essays on Moral Development, Volume 2)*. New York: Harper & Row.

Koskimaa, V., and Rapeli, L. (2015). Political socialization and political interest: The role of school reassessed. *Journal of Political Science Education*, *11*, 141–156. 10.1080/15512169.2015.1016033

Kristofferson, K. (2012). Positive Effects from Negative Virtual Experiences: How Virtual Reality Can Be Used Effectively in Marketing in NA – Advances in Consumer Research Volume 44, Page Moreau and Stefano Puntoni (eds)., pp. 524–525. Duluth, MN.

Kristofferson, K., White, K., and Peloza, J. (2014). The nature of slacktivism: How the social observability of an initial act of token support affects subsequent prosocial action. *Journal of Consumer Research*, *40*, 1149–1166. 10.1086/674137

Kubany, E. S. (1994). A cognitive model of guilt typology in combat-related PTSD. *Journal of Traumatic Stress*, *7*(1), 3–19. 10.1002/jts.2490070103

Kubany, E. S., Haynes, S. N., Abueg, F. R., Manke, F. P., Brennan, J. M., and Stahura, C. (1996). Development and validation of the Trauma-Related Guilt Inventory (TRGI). *Psychological Assessment*, *8*(4), 428–444. 10.1037/1040-3590.8.4.428

Kudrnac, A., and Lyons, P. (2017). Parental example as a motivation for turnout among youths. *Political Studies*, *65*, 43–63. 10.1177/0032321716644614

Lazarsfeld, P. (1966). *Personal Influence: The Part Played by People in the Flow of Mass Communications*. Glencoe, Illinois: Free Press.

Lee, H. (1977). *To Kill a Mockingbird*. London: Arrow.

Luther, L., Rosen, C., Cummins, J. S., and Sharma, R. P. (2020). The multidimensional construct of resilience across the psychosis spectrum: Evidence of alterations in people with early and prolonged psychosis. *Psychiatric Rehabilitation Journal*, *43*(3), 225–233. 10.1037/prj0000393

MacDonald, G. (1867). *Silverhair "The Golden Key"; Golden Hair in Aunt Friendly's Nursery Book*. London: Frederick Warne.

Malm, A., and the Zetkin Collective (2021). *White Skin Black Fuel*. London: Verso.

Manning, N., and Holmes, M. (2014). Political emotions: A role for feelings of affinity in citizens' (dis)engagements with electoral politics? *Sociology – The Journal of the British Sociological Association*, *48*(4), 698–714. 10.1177/0038038

Martin, N. G., Eaves, L. J., Heath, A. C., Jardine, R., Feingold, L., and Eysenck, H. J. (June 1986). Evolution Transmission of social attitudes (attitudes/cultural inheritance/twins/assortative mating/behavior genetics). *Proceedings of the National Academy of Sciences of the United States of America*, *83*, 4364–4368.

Masten, A. S. (2018). Resilience theory and research on children and families: Past, present, and promise. *Journal of Family Theory & Review*, 10, 12–31. 10.1111/jftr.12255

McClelland, D. (1961). *The Achieving Society*. Princeton N.J: Princeton University Press.

McCrae, R. R., and Costa, P. T. (1987). Validation of the five-factor model of personality across instruments and observers. *Journal of Personality and Social Psychology*, *52*(1), 81–90. 10.1037/0022-3514.52.1.81

McCullough, M. E., Kilpatrick, S. D., Emmons, R. A., and Larson, D. B. (2001). Is gratitude a moral affect? *Psychological Bulletin*, *127*(2), 249–266. 10.1037/0033-2909.127.2.249

McKibben, B. (1989). *The End of Nature*. London: Bloomsbury.
Mikes, G. (1946). *How to Be an Alien*. London: Andre Deutsch.
Morozov, E. (2009). The Brave New World of Slacktivism. Foreign Policy (19 May), Available online: http://neteffect.foreignpolicy.com/posts/2009/05/19/the_brave_new_world_of_slacktivism (accessed 27 February 2012).
Mure, E. (1967). *The Story of the Three Bears*. Oxford: Oxford University Press.
Newmann, E. S. (1993). The Brothers Grimm as Collectors and Editors of German Folktales. In D. Haase (ed), *The Reception of Grimms' Fairy Tales: Responses, Reactions, Revisions*, pp. 24–40. Detroit: Wayne State University Press.
Nie, N. H., Verba, S., and Kim, J. (1974). Political participation and the life cycle. *Comparative Politics*, 6, 319–340. 10.2307/421518
Opie, P., and Opie, I. (1974). *The Classic Fairy Tales*. Oxford: Oxford University Press.
Orth, U., Montada, L., and Maercker, A. (2006). Feelings of revenge, retaliation motive, and posttraumatic stress reactions in crime victims. *Journal of Interpersonal Violence*, *21*(2), 229–243. 10.1177/0886260505282286
Orwell, G. (1953). Such were the joys, Harcourt Brace and Company; Boston.
Osmani, V. (2004). "Street Children in Kosovo"; Finnish Human Rights Program in Kosovo in Three Languages (English, Albanian, Serbian).
Osmani, V. (2009). The Big Impact of a Small Program on the Development of Rule of Law in Kosovo (in "The Export of Legal Education: Promoting and Impacting Transition Countries); Ashgate.
Osmani, V. (2011). Balkans - Foreign Affairs, Politics and Socio-Cultures (co-author of section of Kosovo's Foreign Policy); EPOKA University Publications, Tirana; ISBN 978-9928-4044-4-2
Osmani, V. (2013). Kosovo's foreign policy: Five Years On (in "Political Thought: Foreign Policy and Aspects of International Diplomacy", co-author; 2011, No 43, Konrad Adenauer Stiftung).
Osmani, V. (2014). The Role of Parliamentary Diplomacy in Shaping the Foreign Policy of the Republic of Kosovo. University of Pittsburgh, Law Review.
Ozer, E. J., Best, S. R., Lipsey, T. L., Weiss, D. S. (2003). Predictors of posttraumatic stress disorder and symptoms in adults: A meta-analysis. *Psychological Bulletin*, *129*, 52–73.
Patterson, T. E. (2014). Do Children Just Take their Parents' Political Beliefs?The Atlantic May issue.
Payne, L. (1985). A Study of Emotion: Developing Emotional Intelligence; Self-Integration; Relating to Fear, Pain and Desire, Dissertation, The Union for Experimenting Colleges and Universities. Antioch, Ohio.

Perrault, C. (2010). *The Complete Fairy Tales*. Oxford: Oxford University Press.

Philips, D. (2002). Comparative Historical Studies in Education: Problems of Periodisation Reconsidered British Journal of Educational Studies First published: 16 December 2002, 10.1111/1467-8527.t01-1-00208

Piaget, J. (1932). *The Moral Judgment of the Child*. London: Kegan Paul, Trench, Trubner & Co.

Pinker, S. (2011). *The Better Angels of Our Nature a History of Violence and Humanity*. London: Penguin.

Pinker, S. (2019). *Enlightenment Now – the Case for Science, Reason, Humanism and Progress*. London: Penguin.

Quintelier (2017). The effect of political trust and trust in European citizens on European identity. *European Political Science Review*, *9*, 161–181.

Quintelier, E. (2015). Engaging adolescents in politics: The longitudinal effect of political socialization agents. *Youth and Society*, *47*, 51–69. 10.1177/0044118X13507295

Quintelier, E. (2007). Differences in political participation between young and old people. *Contemporary Politics*, *13*, 165–180. 10.1080/13569770701562658

Quintelier, E., and Hooghe, M. (2011). Television and political participation among adolescents: The impact of television viewing, entertainment and information preferences. *Mass Communication and Society*, *14*, 620–642. 10.1080/15205436.2010.530383

Radice, G. (1992). *Southern Discomfort [archive]*. London: Fabian Society.

Rainsford, E. (2017). Exploring youth political activism in the united kingdom: what makes young people politically active in different organisations? *British Journal of Politics and International Relations*, *19*, 790–806. 10.1177/1369148117728666

Rest, J. R. (1979). *Development in Judging Moral Issues*. Minneapolis: University of Minnesota Press.

Ridley, J. (2021). *George V Never a Dull Moment*. London: Chatto and Windus.

Rojas, H., and Puig-i-Abril, E. (2009). Mobilizers mobilized: Information, expression, mobilization and participation in the digital age. *Journal of Computed-Mediated Communication*, 14, 902–927. 10.1111/j.1083-6101.2009.01475.x

Rosen, B. (1980). Moral dilemmas and their treatment. In B. Munsey (ed), *Moral Development, Moral Education, and Kohlberg*, pp. 232–263. Birmingham, Alabama: Religious Education Press.

Salovey, P., and Mayer, J. D. (1990). Emotional Intelligence. *Imagination Cognition and Personality*. 10.2190/DUGG-P24E-52WK-6CDG

Schönpflug, U., and Bilz, L. (2009). *The Transmission Process: Mechanisms and Contexts. Cultural Transmission: Psychological, Developmental,*

Social, And Methodological Aspects. New York, NY: Cambridge University Press.

Scott, P. D. (January 1975). The Tragedy of Maria Colwell. *The British Journal of Criminology*, *15*(1), 88–90, 10.1093/oxfordjournals.bjc.a046614

Shelley, D., and Cohen, D. (1986). *Testing Psychological Tests*. London: Croom Helm.

Southey, R. (2018). *Goldilocks and the Three Bears*. Scotts Valley, California: Create Independent.

Soutter, A. R. B., and Mõttus, R. (2020). Big Five facets' associations with pro-environmental attitudes and behaviors. *Journal of Personality*, *89*, 203–215. 10.1111/jopy.12576

Teixeria, R. (1992). *The Disappearing American Voter*. Washington: Brookings Institution.

Terr, L. C. (1991). Childhood traumas: An outline and overview. *The American Journal of Psychiatry*, *148*(1), 10–20. 10.1176/ajp.148.1.10

Theocharis, Y. (2015). The conceptualization of digitally networked participation. *Social Media and Society*, 1–14. 10.1177/2056305115610140

Theocharis, Y., and van Deth, J. W. (2018a). *Political Participation in a Changing World: Conceptual and Empirical Challenges in the Study of Citizen Engagement*. New York, NY: Routledge. 10.4324/9780203728673

Theocharis, Y., and van Deth, J. W. (2018b). The continuous expansion of citizen participation: A new taxonomy. *European Political Science Review*, *10*, 139–163. 10.1017/S1755773916000230

Timmerman, G. (2009). Youth policy and participation an analysis of pedagogical ideals in municipal youth policy in the Netherlands. *Children and Youth Service Review*, *31*, 572–576. 10.1016/j.childyouth.2008.10.015

Tomasello, M. (2009). *Why We Cooperate*. Cambridge Mass: MIT Press.

Tupes, E. C., and Christal, R. E. (1961). Recurrent Personality Factors based on Trait Ratings.USAF ASD Tech. Rep. No. 61–97, Lackland Airforce Base, TX: US Air Force.

van Deth, J. W. (2001). *Studying Political Participation: Towards a Theory of Everything? Paper presented at the Joint Sessions of Workshops of the European Consortium for Political Research*. Grenoble: ECPR.

van Deth, J. W. (2014). A conceptual map of political participation. *Acta Politica*, *49*, 349–367. 10.1057/ap.2014.6

Van Hiel, A., De Keersmaecker, J., Onraet, E., Haesevoets, T., Roets, A., and Fontaine, J. R. J. (2019). The relationship between emotional abilities and right-wing and prejudiced attitudes. *Emotion*, *19*(5), 917–922. 10.1037/emo0000497 van Deth, J. W., Abendschon, S., and Vollmar, M. (2011). Children and politics: An empirical reassessment of early political socialization. *Political Psychology*, *32*, 147–173. 10.1111/j.1467-9221.2010.00798.x

Verba, S., and Nie, N. H. (1972). *Participation in America. Political Democracy and Social Equality*. New York, NY: Harper and Row.

Wessells, M. (2005). Child soldiers, peace education, and postconflict reconstruction for peace.*Theory Into Practice*, *44*(4), 363–369.

White, W. A. (1917). The theories of Freud, Jung and Adler: III. The Adlerian concept of the neuroses. *The Journal of Abnormal Psychology*, *12*(3), 168.

Wilson, E. O. (1980). *Sociobiology the New Synthesis*. Cambridge, Mass: Harvard University Press.

Winchester, T. M., Binney, W., and Hall, J. (2014). Young adults and politics: Investigating factors influencing voter decision making. *Journal of Nonprofit & Public Sector Marketing*, *26*(3), 226–257. 10.1080/10495142.2014.915635

Young, K. S. (1998a). *Caught in the Net: How to Recognise the Signs of Internet Addiction and a Winning Strategy for Recovery*: New York: Wiley.

Young, K. S. (1998b). Internet addiction: The emergence of a new clinical disorder. *Cyberpsychology and Behaviour*, *1*, 237–244.

Yuen, A. (2007). Discovering children's responses to trauma: A response-based narrative practice. *The International Journal of Narrative Therapy and Community Work*, *4*.

Index